THE AMERICAN KENNEL CLUB'S
Meet the
Miniature
Schnauzer ™

The Responsible Dog Owner's Handbook

AKC's Meet the Breeds Series

I-5
EST 2013
PRESS
I-5 Publishing, LLC™

AN OFFICIAL PUBLICATION OF **AKC** THE AMERICAN KENNEL CLUB

AMERICAN
KENNEL CLUB

Brought to you by The American Kennel Club and the American Miniature Schnauzer Club.
Lead Editor: Andrew DePrisco
Art Director: Cindy Kassebaum
Production Supervisor: Jessica Jaensch
Assistant Production Manager: Tracy Vogtman

I-5 PUBLISHING, LLC™
Chief Executive Officer: Mark Harris
Chief Financial Officer: Nicole Fabian
Vice President, Chief Content Officer: June Kikuchi
General Manager, I-5 Press: Christopher Reggio
Editorial Director, I-5 Press: Andrew DePrisco
Art Director, I-5 Press: Mary Ann Kahn
Digital General Manager: Melissa Kauffman
Production Director: Laurie Panaggio
Production Manager: Jessica Jaensch
Marketing Director: Lisa MacDonald

Copyright © 2014 The American Kennel Club and I-5 Publishing, LLC™

Photographs by: Mary Bloom: 94, 120; Cheryl Ertelt: 18, 69 90-91, 104; Isabelle Francais: 40, 92, 95, 96, 101, 116; Jeannie Harrison/Close Encounters of the Furry Kind: 1, 8, 10, 24, 26, 28-29, 30-31, 33, 39, 45, 46, 70, 78, 98-99, 110-111, 119; Diane Lewis: 3, 6-7, 23, 58, 60, 63, 65, 68, 76, 80, 84, 102, 107; Mark Raycroft Photography: 9, 12, 14, 16-17, 19, 35, 36, 41, 42-43, 49, 51, 52, 55, 56-57, 66-67, 72, 73, 74-75, 82-83, 85, 86, 88, 93, 105, 108, 109, 112, 113, 114, 121; and Shutterstock.com: front cover main image, 89, 97 (Jagodka/Shutterstock.com); front cover insets (Sergey Lavrentev/Shutterstock.com, littleny/Shutterstock.com, Elliot Westacott/Shutterstock.com, AnetaPics/Shutterstock.com); 11, 14 (mariait/Shutterstock.com); 27, 79 (Nikolai Tsvetkov/Shutterstock.com); 32, 47, 118 (Eric Isselee/Shutterstock.com); 48, 62, 81, 124 (Julia Remezova/Shutterstock.com); 71 (stockyimages/Shutterstock.com); 87 (James Clarke/Shutterstock.com); 106 (katielittle/Shutterstock.com); 117 (Vitaly Titov & Maria Sidelnikova/Shutterstock.com); back cover (steamroller_blues/Shutterstock.com).

All rights reserved. No part of this book may be reproduced, stored in a retrieval system, or transmitted in any form or by any means, electronic, mechanical, photocopying, recording, or otherwise, without the prior written permission of I-5 Press™, except for the inclusion of brief quotations in an acknowledged review.

Library of Congress Cataloging-in-Publication Data
The American Kennel Club's meet the Miniature schnauzer : the responsible dog owner's handbook.

    pages cm -- (AKC's meet the breeds series)
  Includes index.
  ISBN 978-1-62008-095-5 (alk. paper)
1. Miniature schnauzer. I. American Kennel Club. II. Title: Meet the Miniature schnauzer.
  SF429.M58A54 2014
  636.76--dc23

                    2013043577

This book has been published with the intent to provide accurate and authoritative information in regard to the subject matter within. While every precaution has been taken in the preparation of this book, the author and publisher expressly disclaim any responsibility for any errors, omissions, or adverse effects arising from the use or application of the information contained herein. The techniques and suggestions are used at the reader's discretion and are not to be considered a substitute for veterinary care. If you suspect a medical problem, consult your veterinarian.

I-5 Publishing, LLC™
3 Burroughs, Irvine, CA 92618
www.facebook.com/i5press
www.i5publishing.com

Printed and bound in the United States
13 14 15 16 17   1 3 5 7 9 8 6 4 2

Meet Your New Dog

Welcome to *Meet the Miniature Schnauzer*. Whether you're a long-time Miniature Schnauzer owner, or you've just gotten your first puppy, we wish you a lifetime of happiness and enjoyment with your new pet.

In this book, you'll learn about the history of the breed, receive tips on feeding, grooming, and training, and learn about all the fun you can have with your dog. The American Kennel Club and I-5 Press hope that this book serves as a useful guide on the lifelong journey you'll take with your canine companion.

Owned and cherished by millions across America, Minis make wonderful companions and also enjoy taking part in a variety of dog sports, including Conformation (dog shows), Obedience, Earthdog events, and Agility.

Thousands of Miniature Schnauzers have also earned the AKC Canine Good Citizen® certification by demonstrating their good manners at home and in the community. We hope that you and your Miniature Schnauzer will become involved in AKC events, too! Learn how to get involved at www.akc.org/events or find a training club in your area at www.akc.org/events/trainingclubs.cfm.

We encourage you to connect with other Mini owners on the AKC website (www.akc.org), Facebook (www.facebook.com/americankennelclub), and Twitter (@akcdoglovers). Also visit the website for the American Miniature Schnauzer Club (www.amsc.us), the national parent club for the Mini, to learn about the breed from reputable exhibitors and breeders.

Enjoy *Meet the Miniature Schnauzer!*
Sincerely,

Dennis B. Sprung
AKC President and CEO

Contents

CHAPTER ONE

Spice Up Your Life

The Miniature Schnauzer will add more than salt and pepper to your life! This colorful little terrier promises to add zest and zing to the life of any true dog lover who's looking for a spunky, confident companion to share his home and heart with. Few can contest the notion that the Miniature Schnauzer is a sharp-looking purebred dog. His hard and wiry outer coat, complete with abundant whiskers and fairly thick fur-

The progenitor of the Miniature Schnauzer was the Standard Schnauzer, a breed that has been used to pull carts, though not necessarily with two Minis aboard!

nishings; his rectangular head, capped by pointed cropped ears or small, folded ears; and his sturdy build cut an unmistakable impression!

WHAT'S IN A NAME!

The breed is "Miniature" in name only: it appears very much like its larger relation, the Standard Schnauzer, and projects no less an air of strength and fearlessness. Much lighter than the Standard, the Miniature Schnauzer weighs less than 20 pounds, but he's a solid, muscular dog who is more rugged than most other terriers and never toyish. For his 12 to 14 inches, he is every inch a watchdog and his family's protector. Minis have no regard for size and feel equal to any dog.

The Miniature Schnauzer, in many ways, is the *un*-terrier of the Terrier Group—perhaps because he's one of the few non-Anglo outsiders of the group or perhaps because he's simply a more reasonable fellow than those feisty Fox Terriers and Scotties. While most other Terriers can be quarrelsome with their own kind—and especially their own sex—Minis can play with other dogs in a nonaggressive manner. They are not fighters, but they will not hesitate to protect themselves when challenged.

Minis are fairly quiet companions compared to many barky ratters and fox-chasers. Like his dirt-loving brethren, the Mini will go to ground after a rat or another pesky varmint, but he's less likely to bolt from his owner's side or wander away from home. Owners, however, are warned that a fence is still an absolute necessity for suburban dwellers, and owners should always keep their Mini on a leash when walking, whether in the country or city.

Miniature Schnauzers can live happily in temperate climates and know how to enjoy the good life on sunny days.

MINIS DON'T CARE ABOUT ZIP CODES

Where you live will matter little to your Miniature Schnauzer. Breeders are happy to place Minis with caring owners who live on Midwestern farms or Texas ranches, canine aficionados in suburban neighborhoods across the country, active beachcombers on either coast, and dog-loving Manhattanites, San Franciscans, Chicagoans, and Austiners alike—as long as he's with a responsible owner, a Mini Schnauzer will be happy.

Even though the schnauzer breeds began as working farm dogs, today's Mini is equally at home in the city, suburbs, or country. He will gladly adapt to any lifestyle his owner chooses for him. It's not uncommon to see Minis being walked along bustling city streets, nor is it uncommon to see these hard-working dogs on large farms and hobby farms. Temperature doesn't much matter to the Mini either, and he'll just as happily join a parade in South Beach as he will a hike in Anchorage. The Mini is adaptable to all terrains and climes, and doesn't mind steps either! If you live on a tenth-floor walkup, you'll be regretting the lack of an elevator long before your Mini does.

Versatility and adaptability are two characteristics that continue to attract new fanciers to the Miniature Schnauzer. As a rule, the Mini is an easy dog to live with. He thrives on companionship and enjoys time spent with his favorite person, whether snoozing on the bed or practicing obedi-

Did You Know?

The Miniature Schnauzer has been bred in the United States since 1925 but took a few decades to make it into the nation's Top Ten breeds. The breed was the number-eight breed for the decades of the 1960s, 1970s, and 1980s, the first time a Terrier breed made the Top Ten since the Smooth Fox was ranked number eight in the 1940s. No Terrier has ever ranked number one for any decade in the AKC's history, though the Airedale Terrier got close during the 1910s, when it was ranked number-two breed in the U.S.

Parent Club

The American Miniature Schnauzer Club was founded in 1933 and is the parent club for twenty-five specialty clubs around the United States. The AMSC has over 600 members in the U.S. The AMSC exists to promote correct type in purebred Miniature Schnauzers, encouraging breeders to conform to the breed standard and for members to participate in formal competitions with their Minis, including conformation, performance, and obedience trials. Educating the public about the proper care and ongoing good health of the breed is of paramount importance to the AMSC.

Puppies inherit their good looks and their outgoing personalities from their parents.

ence lessons. If you already have a family of three children or are expecting to start a family, you needn't worry about the Miniature Schnauzer. He's delighted to take his place alongside human children, accepting them as his playmates and siblings. No matter how tolerant a dog is, though, parents must always ensure that children learn the proper, respectable way to handle and treat a dog. Toddlers and infants, of course, should never be left unsupervised with a dog, for the safety of human and canine alike.

Miniature Schnauzers welcome the attention of children, and the breed's happy outlook on life nicely complements a child's carefree approach to the world. Playing games, chasing a ball or Frisbee, or just running around the backyard are among the many activities that the Mini and his mini playmates can share and enjoy. For the sake of the dog's safety, it's best to teach the children that the dog should chase them instead of their chasing the dog. A dog should never be allowed to think that running away from a human is a good thing. Children are best to play a "come-follow-me" game instead of a "run-for-your-life-little-doggy" game.

The Miniature Schnauzer is the smallest of the three accepted schnauzer breeds. The middle-sized breed, the Standard, is believed to be the original form, dating back to the fifteenth century. The Mini's long résumé of skills can be traced to this versatile progenitor, as the Standard Schnauzer was used as a multipurpose farm dog; a guard dog for home, farm, and property; and a ratter. That these dogs were smart and pleasant to be around made them welcome inside the farmers' homes, not just outside or in the barns. As a member of the Terrier Group, the Miniature Schnauzer's ratting (or mousing) skills remain undiminished to this day, and the alert Mini is willing and able to remove unwanted vermin from

Responsible Pet Ownership

Getting a dog is exciting, but it's also a huge responsibility. That's why it's important to educate yourself on all that is involved in being a good pet owner. As a part of the Canine Good Citizen® test, the AKC has a "Responsible Dog Owner's Pledge," which states:

I will be responsible for my dog's health needs.

- ☐ I will provide routine veterinary care, including checkups and vaccines.
- ☐ I will offer adequate nutrition through proper diet and clean water at all times.
- ☐ I will give daily exercise and regularly bathe and groom.

I will be responsible for my dog's safety.

- ☐ I will properly control my dog by providing fencing where appropriate, by not letting my dog run loose, and by using a leash in public.
- ☐ I will ensure that my dog has some form of identification when appropriate (which may include collar tags, tattoos, or microchip identification).
- ☐ I will provide adequate supervision when my dog and children are together.

I will not allow my dog to infringe on the rights of others.

- ☐ I will not allow my dog to run loose in the neighborhood.
- ☐ I will not allow my dog to be a nuisance to others by barking while in the yard, in a hotel room, etc.
- ☐ I will pick up and properly dispose of my dog's waste in all public areas, such as on the grounds of hotels, on sidewalks, in parks, etc.
- ☐ I will pick up and properly dispose of my dog's waste in wilderness areas, on hiking trails, on campgrounds, and in off-leash parks.

I will be responsible for my dog's quality of life.

- ☐ I understand that basic training is beneficial to all dogs.
- ☐ I will give my dog attention and playtime.
- ☐ I understand that owning a dog is a commitment in time and caring.

A quartet with a little mischief on their minds.

your home, garage, barn, or yard. Likewise, the Mini will also go full tilt at a passing squirrel or rabbit in the field (or around the block), so remember to keep him on leash. Once a terrier's "vermin-alert light" goes on, his "listening ears" naturally turn off.

THE BEST MINI OWNER

Less active owners have frequently shared their couches with Miniature Schnauzers; this dog will happily sit by his owner's side, sharing a box of Amish hard pretzels. However, for the dog's health and fitness (and your own), you're better off keeping your Mini moving and giving him a job to do. The Mini is a dog that was bred to do a job, and he'll just as happily take a pretzel as a reward for a day's work!

This is a smart, mindful breed that likes to please its owner. Minis know how to think and have minds that can easily understand problems and work out solutions. Don't let his size fool you: he's miniature in inches only, not in ambition, desire to work, or intelligence.

Minis are ideal choices for active owners, particularly ones who have a little competitive nature in their blood. Minis like to win! They naturally put their dog smarts and their muscle into a task, which is why you often see Miniature Schnauzers taking home ribbons and titles in the obedience ring. For nearly a hundred years, Miniature Schnauzers have enjoyed a venerable spot in the lives and homes of American dog lovers, and today the breed continues to rank as the most popular terrier in the nation.

Most dog owners defend their breeds' intelligence, but Miniature Schnauzer owners attest to their dogs' near-human intelligence. An exaggeration, perhaps. However, the Miniature Schnauzer breed standard makes a point of including the word "intelligent," and it's one of the few Terrier breed standards to use that word. The Terrier Group as a whole is a bright clan of dogs—the Scottish Terrier is called "thoughtful," the Parson Russell, "clever," and the Wire Fox, "keen of expression"—canine scholars every one, but the Miniature Schnauzer takes it a step further. This dog is able to reason his way through a problem, not by instincts, impulse, or scents, but by *sense*. Minis seem to understand more than your average dog. It is difficult to prove scientifically that the dog is applying any rules of logic to his problem-solving, but he sure makes it look that way.

TAMING THE TERRIER WITHIN

Devotees of the breed often brag that Miniature Schnauzers are easy to train because the dogs are naturally biddable and responsive to obedience work. Most other terriers are too spirited and independent-minded to ever be labeled "easy to train."

The breed's trainability stems from its desire to please its owners. Minis use their own perception to make decisions about the people they meet. They are polite souls who are friendly and calm in the company of people, but they may not accept everyone into their hearts—they have a keen ability to perceive friend or foe, and their memories are long and flawless. Once a Mini has decided that you're one of "his people," however, you are the center of his life. He believes that he understands you, and he needs interaction with his favorite person to remain happy and balanced. It is very easy to communicate with this dog.

Get to Know the AKC

The American Kennel Club, the world's leading canine organization, is dedicated to the betterment and promotion of purebred dogs as family companions. The AKC is the largest dog registry in the United States and was founded in 1884 with the mission of promoting the sport of purebred dogs and breeding for type and function. Supporting everything from health and wellness to fun activities for the whole family, the AKC is committed to advancing the understanding, benefits, and care of all dogs. Help continue the legacy by registering your purebred Miniature Schnauzer with the AKC. It's as simple as filling out the Dog Registration Application you received when you bought your puppy and mailing it in or register online at www.akc.org/dogreg.

AMERICAN KENNEL CLUB®

The Mini's Larger Brethren

The Miniature Schnauzer, a member of the Terrier Group, is the smallest of the three recognized schnauzer breeds; the Giant Schnauzer, standing between 23.5 and 27.5 inches, is the largest; and the Standard Schnauzer, 17.5 to 19.5 inches, is the medium-sized breed. Both the Giant and the Standard Schnauzers are members of the Working Group and were designed to rid vermin from barns, herd, and guard. The Giant also excels in police and military work and was once used to pull carts. Conformationally, all three schnauzers are very similar, though personality-wise they are quite diverse. The two larger breeds only come in pepper and salt and black.

Ten Reasons Minis Make Great Pets

- Compact size, but not fragile or toyish; portable but not breakable
- Intelligent and extremely trainable
- A stylish coat that does not shed
- Playful and affection-ate, but also a competent watchdog
- Fearless and tough, but not aggressive with other dogs
- Unlike other terriers, he is seldom a wanderer
- He will rid your yard and home of unwanted vermin, and can be trained to live with cats and other small pets
- At home anywhere: city, country, suburbs, deserted island, as long as he's with his people
- Untiringly loyal to a favorite person, but loves the whole family
- Not barky or brainlessly vocal, but will sound an alarm when necessary

We know that Miniature Schnauzers are bright little dogs, and they even bark in compound sentences. Although many trainers advise owners to give clear, concise one-word commands, such as "sit," "stay," or "come," not so for a dog as smart as the Mini. This approach is especially useful when teaching the *come* exercise. Use the word "come" to begin an imperative sentence, such as "Come and get this cookie," "Come give mommy a hug," "Come and show me who's a big boy," and, every Miniature Schnauzer's favorite, "Come and get your cheese!" The puppy will associate the word "come" with things he loves: food, affection, and positive reinforcement. Never, ever begin a sentence with "come" for a negative purpose, such as "Come over here right now" or "Come here, you bad girl!"

On the topic of communication, terriers as a whole are an opinionated lot and, as such, frequently have a lot to say. It is fortunate that the Mini Schnauzer is less verbose than most of the other breeds in the Terrier Group, and you can help your dog keep his barking to an appropriate level. No matter how cute you think your Mini Schnauzer pup is when he's yipping, don't encourage him to bark.

Temperament is bred into an animal, but upbringing matters just as much. The breed standard may describe the Miniature Schnauzer as "friendly, intelligent, and willing to please," and most Minis are, but each dog is different. Have you ever noticed how some dog owners always seem to luck out and get perfectly behaved dogs? While good breeding can never be underestimated, obedience training and teaching manners play an equally important role in deciding your dog's nature. Everyone wants a dog who will be a pleasure to have around, one who your friends and family will be happy to see. Don't jeopardize your friendships by exposing your chums to a yappy, needy, whiny dog. Even if he's perfectly handsome, a misbehaving dog is not good company. An owner's responsibility (to the dog and everyone else) is to train his dog to become a true canine good citizen.

THE CULT OF THE SCHNAUZER

Speaking of handsome, the schnauzer breeds may come in various sizes and colors, but there's just one schnauzer! A schnauzer of any size cannot be mistaken for any other dog, purebred or otherwise. The Miniature Schnauzer is at once elegant and handsome, even when his mustached expression conveys a comic air of "grumpy old man." And we know he's anything but a grump! His bushy, thick eyebrows and his full mustache and beard frame his strong, rectangular head and give the Miniature Schnauzer his head-turning stamp. If cropped, the ears add to this distinctive sharp expression, while natural ears soften the

dog's overall look and reflect his mild and easygoing temperament. The Mini's dark eyes impart such intelligence that there is never any doubt that this is a thinking dog.

For all of his good looks and talents, the Miniature Schnauzer's greatest asset is his temperament. As the American Miniature Schnauzer Club's standard describes, the breed "is alert and spirited, yet obedient to command. He is friendly, intelligent, and willing to please." All dog owners agree that there's no dog easier to live with than a happy, affectionate one. The Mini truly lives for his family—whether they're an active family with children or a couple who prefers a quiet life. The Mini will be content in either situation, as long as there's plenty of love—and treats—to go around.

Fun and easy to get along with, Miniature Schnauzers are more dog-friendly than most other terriers and are readily inclined to enjoy the company of other four-legged playmates.

At a Glance ...

Adding a Miniature Schnauzer to your life promises some zest and zing. This little confident dog doesn't know the meaning of the word *miniature,* and his approach to life is big. He knows he's good-looking and that he's a true "keeper."

. . . .

The Miniature Schnauzer is unapologetic about wanting to please his owner. Brighter and more trainable than most of the terriers, the Mini excels in obedience classes and organized sports. Compared to his fellow terriers, he is more mild-mannered and biddable, generally less of a challenge to live with than his feisty earthdog compatriots.

. . . .

Adaptable is the Miniature Schnauzer's middle name. He's happy to live in any area of the nation, from east to west, north to south, in cities, suburbs, or farms. The ideal owner for the naturally friendly and outgoing Mini is someone who will spend time with the dog, training him, grooming him, and interacting with him. His mind is as active as his body.

CHAPTER TWO

The Making of a Schnauzer

Miniature Schnauzers are essentially a twentieth-century creation, even though the breed's progenitor, the Standard Schnauzer, can be traced back to fifteenth-century artwork and literary references. By the early 1900s, the Miniature Schnauzer was being registered as a purebred dog. By the 1920s, American breeder Marie Slattery began importing dogs from German breeder Rudolph

All Miniature Schnauzers in the United States today can trace their family trees back to three foundation dogs.

Krappatsch to form the illustrious Marienhof Kennel, which became the foundation of the breed in the United States. For over half a century, Marienhof produced champion Miniature Schnauzers, over one hundred in all. By the time the Dorem Kennels of Dorothy Williams came along in the 1940s, the breed was a recognizable purebred, a celebrated show dog, and a favorite pet in the United States. For the second half of the twentieth century, the Miniature Schnauzer ranked in the American Kennel Club's Top Ten breeds, reaching a high of number five for three consecutive years, from 1969 to 1971.

It's easy to understand the breed's popularity in America and around the world. A list of the breed's assets reads like a heartfelt Valentine. The Mini is handsome and well dressed in his crisp, perfectly fitted coat. He doesn't look like other dogs: he's unique, with a face that goes beyond "cute" and "sweet." He's a sensitive, emotionally available companion,

A PIECE OF HISTORY

One of three German sires stand on the extreme left of every Miniature Schnauzer pedigree. The black dog Peter v. Westerberg, the salt and pepper dog Lord v. Dornbusch, and the bicolor or black and silver dog Prinz v. Rheinstein are the foundation of the breed and also represent the three acceptable colors in Miniature Schnauzers today.

happy to live in any environment or climate. On top of all that, he's a hard worker and one of the smartest dogs around, highly regarded for his trainability and willingness to please. In Ira Gershwin's famous rhetoric, "Who could ask for anything more?"

HE'S TOTALLY YOUR TYPE...AND HIS

Of course, the Miniature Schnauzer's good looks, smarts, and personality are not by accident. They are, in fact, by design. When you visit (or view on television or online) the Westminster Kennel Club dog show in New York City or the famous Montgomery County Kennel Club all-terrier show in Pennsylvania, it's not by serendipity that all ten or one hundred Miniature Schnauzers possess extremely similar characteristics: small, dark eyes; a well-arched neck; straight front legs; slanting thighs; sloping shoulders; round feet; and the same silhouette in profile as you pan down the line-up. A breed's type—essentially the sum of the parts that give a breed its particular look—is the result of breeders' all using the same "recipe." This recipe is called a breed standard, a menu of features describing a particular breed of dog. From the tip of the nose to the end of the tail, a breed standard paints an expert portrait of an individual dog.

Every breed of dog recognized by the American Kennel Club (AKC) has a breed standard that was drawn up by its national breed club, called the parent club, and then approved and accepted by the AKC. The parent club for the Miniature Schnauzer in the United States, the American Miniature Schnauzer Club (AMSC), is the author and protector of the breed standard, and it encourages all breeders to abide by the specific details in the standard. For this reason, all Miniature Schnauzers in the show

Affenpinschers

Although the smart Affenpinschers we see in AKC show rings today could never be confused with our equally snazzy but distinctive Miniature Schnauzers, these two breeds were once simply called "small or dwarf wirehaired pinschers." The Germans referred to these little dogs as Rauhhaarige Zwergpinschers. By 1900 the Zwergpinschers were divided by size: the toy-sized dogs were Affenpinschers, and the larger dogs were Miniature Schnauzers. The dogs were officially recognized as distinct breeds by the German Kennel Club in 1910.

Regardless of the color of the dog, Miniature Schnauzers are bred to the same standard.

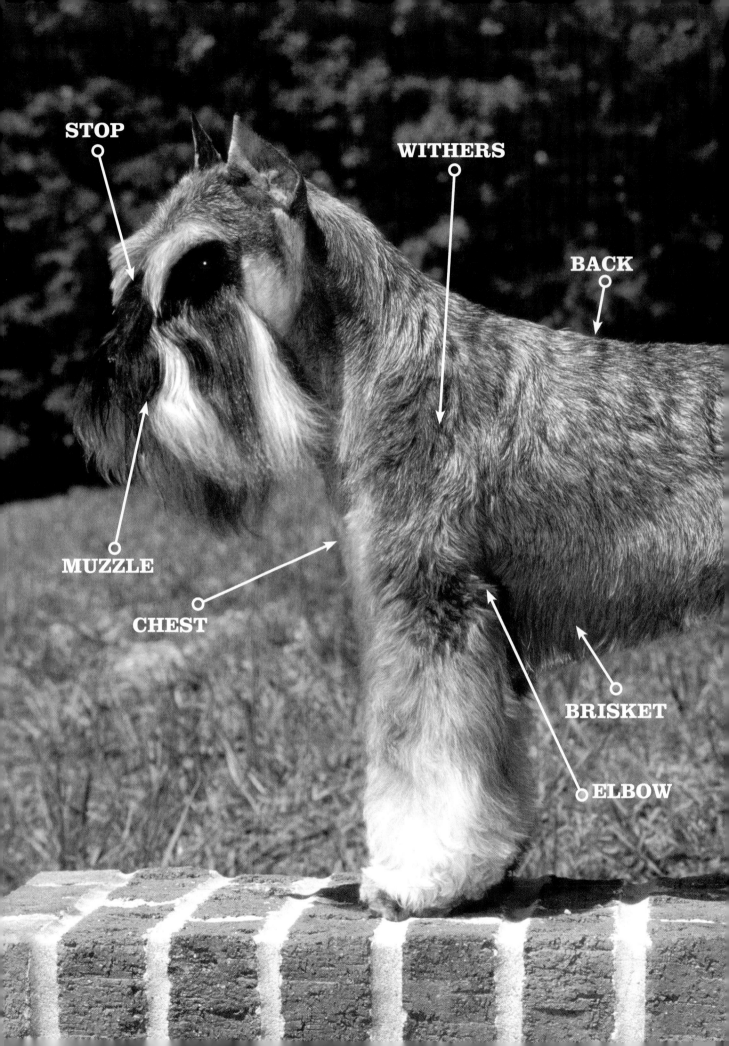

STOP

WITHERS

BACK

MUZZLE

CHEST

BRISKET

ELBOW

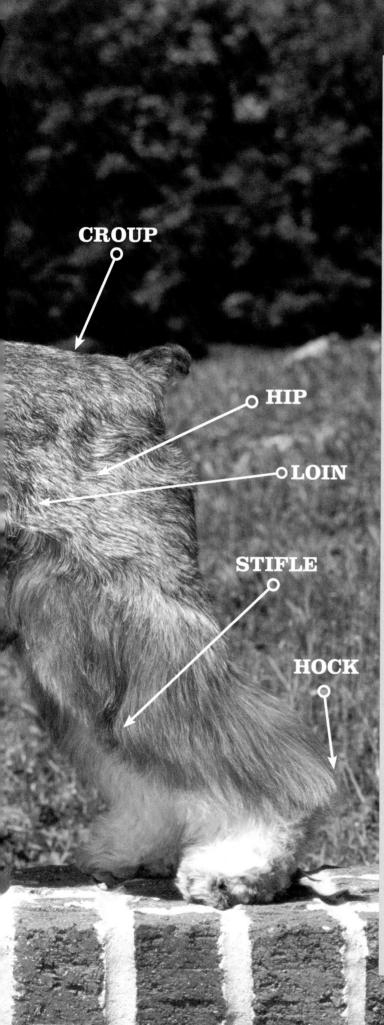

CROUP

HIP

LOIN

STIFLE

HOCK

The Miniature Schnauzer in Brief

COUNTRY OF ORIGIN:
Germany

ORIGINAL USE:
Ratting, guard duty, companionship

AVERAGE LIFE SPAN:
14 to 16 years

COAT:
A double coat, with a hard, wiry outer coat

COLORS:
Salt and pepper, black and silver, solid black

GROOMING:
Brush the coat weekly; wipe the furnishings clean. Clipper the pet Mini or hand-strip the coat every two to three months to maintain its proper texture.

HEIGHT/WEIGHT:
12 to 14 inches; 11 to 20 pounds

TRAINABILITY:
Better than most terriers!

PERSONALITY:
Alert and spirited; smart but willing to please; affectionate and sweet; the classic one-person dog.

ACTIVITY LEVEL:
Moderate. Minis love to play with their owners and are super adaptable, making the breed an excellent choice for urban dog lovers. Daily exercise, in the form of romps in a fenced yard or on-leash walks, is mandatory.

GOOD WITH OTHER PETS:
Minis love other dogs and, with socialization, will accept cats, too. Small-mammal pets, such as hamsters and guinea pigs, are not safe around this terrier breed.

NATIONAL BREED CLUB:
American Miniature Schnauzer Club; www.amsc.us

RESCUE:
Visit the parent club's website and select the "Rescue" tab for more information.

The Miniature Schnau-
zer is already a minia-
turized version of the
Standard Schnauzer, so
what is the allure of the
Toy Schnauzer? In fact,
there is no such thing as
a Toy Schnauzer. Re-
sponsible breeders do
not breed overly small
dogs to attain dogs that
do not meet the height
requirements in the
breed standard. The
standard states that
dogs under 12 inches at
the shoulder are dis-
qualified and states that
"toyishness" in type is a
fault. Undersized dogs
can be as small as 10
inches. The Miniature
Schnauzer is a member
of the Terrier Group and
was never intended to
be a Toy dog.

ring fall within the 12-to-14-inch range and possess one of three accepted coat colors. A breed standard can change from time to time if a given feature requires further clarification or as the breed itself changes and "improves."

The Miniature Schnauzer's coat is described in the breed standard as "double, with hard, wiry outer coat and close undercoat." Like most other Terrier breeds, the Mini requires plucking (or stripping) of the coat to retain the desired hardness and wiry feel. The standard specifies that the "head, neck, ears, chest, tail, and body coat must be plucked." While many owners of pet Mini Schnauzers opt to have their dogs clippered for easy maintenance, the electric buzzer changes the breed's desired coat texture. It's easiest to keep a pet Mini tidily groomed year 'round; stripped coats go through shaggy stages. A Miniature Schnauzer's ideal show coat should be "of sufficient length to determine texture," which means not too short or long on the body. The coat on the neck, ears, and skull is shorter than the rest of the body, and the furnishings on the legs and face are "fairly thick but not silky."

The late all-breed judge Anna Katherine Nicholas praised the Miniature Schnauzer breed standard for the specificity of its language, which she felt gave judges and breeders a clear picture of the correct Mini. In the ring, Miss Nicholas looked for "a beautifully proportioned, square-ly built, solid little dog with good bone and substance; a short straight back which slopes slightly downward from the withers (highest point of shoulder) to the tail; and an overall appearance of solidity."

It's also difficult to overlook a beautiful head in the show ring. "Miniature Schnauzers have strong, rectangular heads which taper slightly in width from ears to eyes to tip of nose. The skull is flat on top and moderately long, the foreface parallel to the skull, or *at least* equal length, with a slight stop. The muzzle should never be too pointed, or 'snipy,' but ends rather like a blunt wedge..."

The breed standard also describes the gait of an ideal Mini, and Miss Nicholas explains it from a judge's point of view: "As you watch a Miniature Schnauzer move, the forelegs should reach well out; the hindlegs flex nicely and powerfully at stifle and hock joint. Forelegs and hindlegs should travel in the same planes as each other, neither too close nor too far apart." In the show ring, a Mini should trot, never gallop, to show off his best.

TRUE SCHNAUZER COLORS

The most common color in the Miniature Schnauzer is salt and pepper. This popular and instantly recognizable color appears essentially as a shaded gray, created by the combination of black-and-white banded hairs with solid black hairs and solid white hairs. The darkest coloration is on the back and sides of the dog, becoming light gray to silvery white on parts of the face and extremities. Because a salt and pepper dog's hairs are banded, the more black in each individual hair, the darker the dog appears.

The black and silver coloration follows the same pattern as the salt and pepper: the back and sides of the dog are black, with lighter mark-

What's a "Bentchur"?

Canine literature refers to a dog called a bentchur, which was described as having a "snout covered with rough-haired whiskers.....
His body is short, and his tail is usually docked. The topcoat is not too long but wiry..." The word pinscher may derive from the word bentchur, though cynologists later translated pinscher to mean terrier, which limits the meaning of the word and the function of the dogs. The word schnauzer derives from the nickname for the dog with a long snout or "schnauze" in German. A wirehaired pinscher from the Wurttenberg kennel of C. Berger named "Schnauzer" won first place at the third International Dog Show in Hanover in 1879. At ensuing shows, the wirehaired pinschers were called Schnauzers. Count Henri van Bylandt, an international dog show judge regarded as the father of the Poodle standard, was the first to refer to the dwarf wirehaired pinscher as the Zwergschnauzer in print: his landmark volume *Les Races des Chien* was published in 1894 and appeared in various languages and subsequent editions.

Minis are active and energetic little dogs who thrive on plenty of outdoor activity. Always encourage your Mini to chase you around the yard: never chase your dog in play.

ings on the eyebrows, muzzle furnishings, cheeks, neck, chest, underside of the tail, front and hind leg furnishings, and underside of the body. The lighter coloration of the underbody should not extend higher than the dog's front elbows. A black and silver dog has a black undercoat.

The black Miniature Schnauzer is a true black, with solid black hairs on the entire body, including the furnishings and undercoat. A black dog may have a small white spot on the chest or an individual white hair here and there. Black dogs should not have brownish coloration anywhere on the body, though the whiskers can become tinged from eating.

If you ever have the chance to see a litter of newborn Mini Schnauzer puppies, you would notice that the salt and pepper may appear almost black or blackish and fawn at birth. Within two or three weeks, gray or brown coloration begins to appear at the roots, and tan markings may be visible on the ears, under the nose, and on the chin, prior to the whiskers' growing longer. Light spots over each eye precede those trademark schnauzer eyebrows, which start to grow in at around six weeks of age. Black and silver Minis are born solid black except for little spots over their eyes, cheeks, and chins. They may be born with taupe on lower legs and feet, too.

ENTER THE EARTH DOGS

The breeds classified in the Terrier Group are those dogs that were bred to rid the countryside (a.k.a. barns, basements, and backyards) of vermin. The terriers' quarry ranges from the tiny field mouse (that even a spoiled housecat could handle) and rats (ranging in size from mouselike to catlike!) to foxes and otters, both crafty and vicious when pursued. Dogs bred to go after these pesky critters need to be tough as nails and able to think on their toes. When you're deep in a foxhole, you better be able to make decisions for yourself and not have to rely on your handler, who's above ground and 20 feet away. Terriers are designed to make up their minds and act swiftly, especially when on the job. They also move as fast as they think, which saves their lives in many cases.

All terriers are feisty and bold by nature, though, of course, every dog is different. The various terrier breed standards describe the desired temperaments as "courageous and self-reliant" (West Highland White Terrier), "tenacious and single minded" (Parson Russell Terrier), "with a confident cock-of-the-walk attitude" (Lakeland Terrier), and "rugged and stout-hearted" (Irish Terrier). The similarity of temperaments among the breeds in the group is apparent, but equally important is a terrier's loyalty to and affection for his owner, as well as his good nature and friendly demeanor.

Terriers as a rule are not the most dog-friendly canines, and some breeds are sparred in the show ring to demonstrate their gameness. The bull-and-terrier breeds, such as the Bull Terrier and the Staffordshire Bull Terrier, are prized for their "indomitable courage" and fearlessness.

Most terriers have hard, wire coats, but there are exceptions to every rule— namely, the Soft Coated Wheaten Terrier (silky and soft) and the Bedlington Terrier (a crisp combo of hard and soft). Even the coats of

Pinscher vs. Schnauzer

The name Pinscher translates in German as terrier, though gripper or grabber is also an apt translation of the German word. Pinschers are known to grab and bite their prey. The pinscher and schnauzer breeds share a long history, and early German breeders would divide puppies in a litter by their coat type, referring to the smooth-coated pups as pinschers and the wire-coated pups as schnauzers. The German Pinscher-Schnauzer Klub prohibited interbreeding between the two types in 1923. The pepper and salt color, so prominent in schnauzers, is disqualified in the German Pinscher today.

Join the Club

The national breed club or parent club of a breed is considered the expert on everything related to that breed of dog. It's responsible for safeguarding and promoting a particular dog breed. These national organizations are members of the American Kennel Club and are made up of knowledgeable breeders and owners. Each parent club determines the breed standard, denoting the traits of an ideal specimen of the breed, which the American Kennel Club then officially approves. The standard is used to guide breeding practices and competition judging. The parent club of the Miniature Schnauzer is the American Miniature Schnauzer Club, founded in 1933. Learn more about the club and its history at its website, www.amsc.us.

The Miniature Schnauzer Breed Standard

AMERICAN
KENNEL CLUB®

GENERAL APPEARANCE: The Miniature Schnauzer is a robust, active dog of terrier type, resembling his larger cousin, the Standard Schnauzer, in general appearance, and of an alert, active disposition.

SIZE, PROPORTION, SUBSTANCE

Size—From 12 to 14 inches. He is sturdily built, nearly square in proportion of body length to height with plenty of bone, and without any suggestion of toyishness.

HEAD

Eyes—Small, dark brown and deepset. They are oval in appearance and keen in expression. Ears—When cropped, the ears are identical in shape and length with pointed tips. They are in balance with the head and not exaggerated in length. They are set high on the skull and carried perpendicularly at the inner edges, with as little bell as possible along the outer edges. When uncropped, the ears are small and V-shaped, folding close to the skull. Head—Strong and rectangular, its width diminishing slightly from ears to eyes, and again to the tip of the nose. The forehead is unwrinkled. The topskull is flat and fairly long. The foreface is parallel to the topskull, with a slight stop, and it is at least as long as the topskull. The muzzle is strong in proportion to the skull; it ends in a moderately blunt manner, with thick whiskers which accentuate the rectangular shape of the head. The teeth meet in a scissors bite.

NECKLINE, TOPLINE, BODY

Neck—Strong and well arched, blending into the shoulders, and with the skin fitting tightly at the throat. Body—Short and deep, with the brisket extending at least to the elbows. Ribs are well sprung and deep, extending well back to a short loin. The underbody does not present a tucked up appearance at the flank. The backline is straight; it declines slightly from the

withers to the base of the tail. The withers form the highest point of the body. The overall length from chest to buttock appears to equal the height at the withers. Tail—Set high and carried erect. It is docked only long enough to be clearly visible over the backline of the body when the dog is in proper length of coat. A properly presented Miniature Schnauzer will have a docked tail as described; all others should be severely penalized.

FOREQUARTERS

Forelegs are straight and parallel when viewed from all sides. They have strong pasterns and good bone. They are separated by a fairly deep brisket which precludes a pinched front. The elbows are close. The sloping shoulders are muscled, yet flat and clean. They are well laid back. Both the shoulder blades and upper arms are long, permitting depth of chest at the brisket. Feet short and round (cat feet) with thick, black pads. The toes are arched and compact.

HINDQUARTERS

The hindquarters have strong-muscled, slanting thighs. They are well bent at the stifles. There is sufficient angulation so that, in stance, the hocks extend beyond the tail. The hindquarters never appear overbuilt or higher than the shoulders. The rear pasterns are short and, in stance, perpendicular to the ground and, when viewed from the rear, are parallel to each other.

COAT

Double, with hard, wiry, outer coat and close undercoat. Close covering on neck, ears, and skull. Furnishings are fairly thick but not silky.

—Excerpts from the American Miniature Schnauzer Club Breed Standard

breeds such as the Smooth Fox Terrier and the Bull Terrier should be hard and "harsh to the touch," even though they are smoother than wire-coated terriers such as the Lakeland, Welsh, and Wire Fox.

Generally speaking, the Terriers aren't large dogs, with the tallest, the Airedale Terrier, at 23 inches at the shoulder; and, the shortest, the Norfolk Terrier, at 10 inches. The Miniature Schnauzer, 12 to 14 inches, is on the lower end of the height range in the group.

Nearly all of the breeds in the Terrier Group hail from the British Isles. That's not to say that all of the world's vermin dwell in England, Scotland, Ireland, and Wales, but rather to say that the English, Scottish, Irish, and Welsh were crafty enough to solve their vermin problem by creating the world's best terriers. There are plenty of rodents elsewhere on the planet...and mostly inferior dogs chasing them! Of course, there is one outstanding exception: the Miniature Schnauzer of Germany.

The Miniature Schnauzer's nose must be solid black, even as puppies.

At a Glance ...

Devised in the 1900s, the Miniature Schnauzer remains one of the most popular and recognizable purebred dogs in the world. Snazzy and mannerly, Minis have it all and are happy to share their positive assets with their devoted people.

. . . .

That all well-bred Miniature Schnauzers look alike is no accident: the breed standard defines the type, size, movement, and temperament that breeders strive for in the whelping box and judges seek in the show ring.

. . . .

The Miniature Schnauzer belongs to the AKC's Terrier Group. The breed is one of the few that do not derive from the British Isles.

. . . .

In black and white (salt and pepper) and shades of grey, the Miniature is only figuratively colorful. Avoid "innovative" breeders attempting to sell wrong-colored Minis.

CHAPTER THREE

Choosing a Mini Puppy

You're ready to start your search for a Miniature Schnauzer puppy. Unlike the purchase of a new car or a new dining room table, the search for a new puppy will require some research, decision-making, and patience. Your choice of the Miniature Schnauzer is very specific: you've selected this breed from all of the recognized American Kennel Club breeds, decided upon a Terrier, and zoomed into

the Miniature Schnauzer. Now we begin to make some more specific decisions—sex, color, background—and locate the very best possible Miniature Schnauzer that possesses all of the characteristics you admire in this breed.

FIRST LET'S TALK ABOUT SEX

The sex of a new baby is the first question most new parents ponder, and many soon-to-be dog owners do, too. Do you want a girl or a boy? Biological mothers and fathers don't have a choice in the matter, but dog parents do! A female dog (bitch) and a male dog (dog) each presents his or her own unique advantages, though every dog is different. Many breeders will tell you that males are more affectionate and devoted, but that's not to say that every dog will be more affectionate than a sweetheart bitch. Likewise, we hear that males are more territorial and tend to wander. There will always be that bitch that insists on being the home protector or who's never happy staying at home, and there's always a dog who is easygoing and content to just chill at home and not bother with seeking out adventures or serendipitous romances.

If you are planning on showing your Miniature Schnauzer, many people recommend starting out with a male dog so you don't have to deal with a bitch's monthly estrous cycle. Some males may be more challenging to train than females, but, again, this depends on the dog, the trainer, and how many treats you're willing to hand over for a nice long sit. If, on the other hand, you're wishing to become a breeder, a bitch is the only way to go. Depending on where you live and the breeder you choose, the price could be the same or higher for one sex or the other.

If choosing a pet, pick the puppy with the personality you like, don't worry about the sex.

IT'S ESSENTIALLY BLACK AND WHITE

Most new owners are looking for a Mini in salt and pepper, long the most popular color. The breed, as we've noted, also comes in solid black and black and silver, both of which are also attractive. Don't get confused by searching online and discovering additional color variations in the breed. Solid white is the most common "other" color you will see, and while it is an acceptable color in Europe, it is not able to be shown in the U.S. except in obedience and agility.

Sadly, some very "colorful" breeders have attempted to widen the color spectrum with hues and patterns of their own. "New" colors such as chocolate and liver and "rare" patterns such as sable,

particolor, and merle are being promoted on the Internet by breeders who choose to march to their own drummers. Salt and pepper Minis that have been machine-clipped often appear silver, though this is not actually a color in the breed. Oftentimes, Miniature Schnauzers of unrecognized colors are on the small size, likely pointing to crossbreeding with toy breeds to achieve the desired color or pattern. While there is some evidence that certain colors have remained recessive in the breed for generations, these unusual colors are more directly the result of breeding Minis to silver Affenpinschers, belge Brussels Griffons, and West Highland White Terriers. The AMSC warns that buyers should never pay a premium for a Miniature Schnauzer because of his color, and they emphasize the importance of preserving the true colors of the breed.

WHAT TO LOOK FOR

Every puppy, no matter the breed, should be *alert* and *friendly*, and of course those two words are used in the Miniature Schnauzer breed standard. They well describe a healthy puppy. Young Mini puppies should feel solid with good bone when you feel them and pick them up. Minis of all ages have good appetites. They should be active and play vigorously with their siblings. The newborn's coat is short and smooth, but by the time you visit the litter, around six weeks, it should begin to change. This new puppy coat is usually darker than the adult's coat will be, with salt and

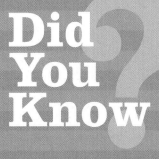

Did You Know

The Miniature Schnauzer, a dog of German descent, was the only breed in the Terrier Group that didn't hail from the British Isles, and the breed retained that distinction for eighty-five years until the Cesky Terrier, from the Czech Republic, was admitted in 2011.

peppers looking just slightly lighter than the black and black and silvers. Black puppies are born black, including their undercoats.

Young Miniature Schnauzer puppies appear somewhat out of proportion, with their heads too large and their legs too short. Often, a puppy's body is a bit heavy for his legs, and the puppy will have to shift his weight to his hindquarters to adjust. Puppies don't have the smooth gait that adult dogs should have. By eight to ten weeks, the puppy's body loses that roly-poly look, and the legs catch up to his frame. Soon the puppy will look like a shrunken-down version of an adult dog, usually by around twelve weeks of age, and he will be moving with more coordination and grace. The Miniature Schnauzer is a fast-growing little breed and usually attains its full height (give or take an inch) by six to eight months of age. Smaller Minis tend to mature faster than larger ones. The puppy will continue to fill out and develop musculature until he's a year old.

A typical, sound puppy should have:
- Good bone and a solid feel to the body
- Lots of whiskers sprouting from the muzzle
- Dark brown eyes, medium sized and oval shaped
- Medium-small ears that fold close to the head
- Puppy teeth in a scissors bite (not over- or undershot)
- A clean resilient puppy coat that is flat and smooth
- Straight front legs, and hind legs that angle toward the hock (ankle)

RECOGNIZING A GOOD BREEDER

Most people recognize the Miniature Schnauzer. This breed cannot be mistaken for the other terriers, and his distinct coloration, face, and overall schnauzer look set him apart. Minis are popular all over the country, and many people remember a Mini from childhood, whether a family pet or one owned by a favorite aunt, a neighbor, or a family friend. Since there's never been a shortage of Miniature Schnauzers, finding a litter of puppies should not pose much difficulty in most parts of the United States. That said, it may be more difficult to locate a good breeder who's producing the kind of Miniature Schnauzer puppy you have your mind, heart, and eye set on.

Miniature Schnauzers are versatile dogs who can serve a variety of purposes in addition to companionship: if you would like a Mini for obedience or agility competition, you'll have to find a breeder whose dogs have excelled in these areas. Because companionship comes natural to the Mini, a career in therapy work may be ahead of any well-bred and well-socialized Miniature Schnauzer. Mini owners will find that visiting seniors in retirement homes or rehab centers is greatly rewarding.

When looking for a breeder, the health of the dogs should be your primary consideration. All breeds of dog and mixed breeds are susceptible to congenital diseases, and responsible breeders screen their dogs prior to breeding. Thanks to the dedication of responsible breeders who track the health of their breeding stock, we know the prevalence for certain diseases in specific breeds of dog.

Enrolled in the AKC Canine Health Information Center (CHIC), the AMSC has adopted a very active stance on preventive measures to ward off hereditary diseases in the Miniature Schnauzer. The club requires member breeders to screen puppies and young adults for eye conditions as well as mitral valve disease, and it recommends myotonia testing. The CHIC database provides statistical information on disease prevalence within a breed so that breeders can take action before a disease becomes widespread and possibly debilitating for the entire breed population.

Eye conditions: Breeders should have the eyes of all potential breeding stock tested for cataracts, retinal dysplasia (RD), and progressive retinal atrophy (PRA). Retinal dysplasia in Miniature Schnauzers is a recessive gene inherited from both parents. The type of PRA that occurs in the Miniature Schnauzer is called photoreceptor dysplasia (pd) and is unique to the breed.

A responsible breeder will have the eyes of both parents and the puppies screened for congenital disorders.

As mentioned, the AMSC stresses to breeders the importance of having their puppies eye-tested prior to sale by a board-certified canine ophthalmologist. Visit the AMSC's website (http://amsc.us) for the most up-to-date information about eye screening for sires and dams, as well as certification from the Canine Eye Registration Foundation (CERF) or the Orthopedic Foundation for Animals (OFA).

Heart condition: Once the Miniature Schnauzer is a year old, a board-certified veterinary cardiologist should perform a stethoscope exam to determine the presence or absence of mitral valve disease, the result of which should be submitted to the cardiac registry or the OFA.

Other possible concerns: Myotonia congenita is a hereditary disorder of the bones and muscles that affects a dog's ability to move and eat normally; DNA testing is available, and only "clear" dogs (neither affected nor carriers of the gene) should be considered for breeding. High fat levels in Miniature Schnauzers, known as hyperlipidermia, increases a dog's chances of developing pancreatitis as well as diabetes mellitus. Overweight

A Tail of Two Schnauzers

The puppy's tail is customarily docked at three days of age. Although other countries, including Germany and England, have outlawed tail docking, Americans continue to dock tails. The AMSC breed standard states that the tail "is docked only long enough to be clearly visible over the backline of the body when the dog is in proper length of coat." Dogs presented without a correctly docked tail should be severely penalized by the judge.

middle-aged Minis are most at risk. Urinary stones are not uncommon in Miniature Schnauzers.

MEETING THE BREEDER

As you've been glancing through these pages, you probably are very excited to meet a puppy as cute as the ones captured by our photographers. Patience is required when acquiring a puppy. The acquisition can take longer than expected, especially if you have to wait for a litter to be born. You have to be certain about the puppy's temperament and overall health; otherwise, you will pay for it many times over, financially and emotionally.

Trusting the breeder you choose is very important. How do you find a

Get Your Registration and Pedigree

A responsible breeder will be able to provide your family with an American Kennel Club registration form and pedigree.

AKC REGISTRATION: When you buy a Miniature Schnauzer from a breeder, ask the breeder for an American Kennel Club Dog Registration Application form. The breeder will fill out most of the application for you. When you fill out your portion of the document and mail it to the AKC, you will receive a Registration Certificate, proving that your dog is officially part of the AKC. Besides recording your name and your dog's name in the AKC database, registration helps fund the AKC's good works, such as canine health research, search-and-rescue teams, educating the public about responsible dog care, and much more.

CERTIFIED PEDIGREE: A pedigree is an AKC certificate that proves your dog is a purebred. It shows your puppy's family tree, listing the names of his parents and grandparents. If your dog is registered with the AKC, the organization will have a copy of your dog's pedigree on file, which you can order from its website (www.akc.org). Look for any titles that your Miniature Schnauzer's ancestors have won, including Champion (conformation), Companion Dog (obedience), and so forth. A pedigree doesn't guarantee the health or personality of a dog, but it's a starting point for picking out a good Miniature Schnauzer puppy.

breeder who will offer you a sound, healthy puppy as well as advice and encouragement throughout your Mini Schnauzer's life? Every prospective dog owner should begin his or her puppy search at www.akc.org. The American Kennel Club's website provides information on every breed of dog recognized by the club plus links to the parent clubs' sites. The AKC also has a Breeder of Merit program, and only experienced breeders who meet set qualifications can be enrolled. Knowing that a breeder has been "in" Miniature Schnauzers for more than five years and has bred (or co-bred) more than ten champions offers comfort to puppy buyers. Anyone can breed a litter of puppies—most dogs breed naturally and can rear their own pups—but good breeders know which dogs to breed together (and which ones not to breed).

The goal of a good breeder is always to improve the breed; financial gain is secondary. Breeding dogs the correct way is an expensive endeavor. The veterinary care, feeding, and rearing of the dam and her litter (for at least eight weeks) is costly. Money is never the main goal of a good breeder, and oftentimes a breeder loses money on a litter. A breeder will set a fair price for a pet puppy, which should be considerably less than the price for a show puppy. A pet puppy from a good breeder is just as healthy and sound as a show puppy, and the "pet" designation reflects the breeder's opinion that the pup's conformation is lacking in one way

It doesn't take an expert to recognize quality in a well-bred Miniature Schnauzer puppy. Look at the coats, attitude, and facial expression of this dynamic duo.

The sire and dam of your chosen litter must be registered with the AKC in order for your puppy to be registered. Get all of the required paperwork from the breeder before completing your transaction.

Why Should You Register with the American Kennel Club?

Registering your puppy with the American Kennel Club helps the AKC do many good things for dogs everywhere, such as promote responsible breeding and support the care and health of dogs throughout the country. As a result of your registration, the AKC is able to inspect kennels across the country, educate dog owners about the importance of training through the Canine Good Citizen® Program, support search-and-rescue canines via the AKC Companion Animal Recovery Canine Support and Relief Fund, teach the public about the importance of responsible dog ownership through publications and the annual AKC Responsible Dog Ownership Days, and much more. Not only is the AKC a respected organization dedicated to the purebred dog, but it is also devoted to the well-being of all dogs everywhere. For more information, visit www.akc.org.

or another—minor aesthetic details that are inconsequential to pet owners. Ears that are set a tad low or a snout that is a wee bit too short have no effect on a pet's overall soundness, handsome schnauzer looks, and personality. As long as the puppy is healthy and his temperament is reliable, you're on your way to a happy life with your Mini.

LET'S PLAY 20 QUESTIONS!

When you meet a breeder, be ready to answer a lot of questions, and have your own list of questions, too. Most breeders will begin by asking you whether or not you've owned a Miniature Schnauzer, or any dog, before. If you grew up with dogs in your home, or Minis particularly, the breeder will be happy to know that you're experienced. When the breeder asks you how long your previous dogs lived, he or she hopes that you have the answer. The breeder definitely doesn't want to hear you say, "I don't know because we gave the dog away when he was three." The breeder really wants to make sure that your home is suitable for one of his or her progeny. Breeders invest lots of money and love into every puppy, and it's their primary concern to find the right permanent homes for their "kids."

The breeder will ask you about your home life and whether you live in a house, condo, or apartment; whether you have children and how old they are; whether you have a fenced yard; and whether everyone in the house is in favor of getting a puppy. The breeder hopes that you will provide a safe, controlled environment for the puppy.

If the breeder has no questions for you, don't think that you're lucky. The more thorough the breeder's interrogation of you, the better a breeder he or she likely is, which means the better the puppies will likely be. A breeder who doesn't care about what type of owner you will be or what kind of home you can provide is likely more interested in whether you're paying by cash or check than in the puppy's well-being.

You must have some questions for the breeder, too. Don't feel like you're bothering the breeder by asking questions. A good breeder will be glad that you're being thorough in your selection of a puppy.

- How long have you been breeding Minis? Do you breed any other breeds?
- Why did you choose this dam to breed? What makes her special?
- How did you choose her mate?
- What hereditary diseases do you screen for? Can you explain how CERF or OFA works? Have you had any health problems with your dogs in the past?
- May I have a copy of the sales contract? What guarantees do you offer to puppy buyers?
- Can you give me a list of some owners who have your puppies?
- Are both parents registered with the American Kennel Club? Have you registered the litter?

Starting a Puppy Folder

Here's the list of all of the paperwork you need to take home with you. Discuss all of these with your breeder before you pick up your puppy.

• A certified AKC pedigree

• AKC papers to individually register your dog

• Veterinary information about the pup's vaccinations and a recommended schedule to review with your veterinarian

• Feeding recommendations, including the breeder's personal advice about which puppy food is best

• A written sales agreement

• Certificates showing that the parents and puppy have been cleared by OFA and CERF

• Breeder's contact information for any follow-up questions or concerns that arise

• Do you show your own dogs? How many champions have you bred? Is the sire of the litter a champion?
• Have any of your dogs been used as therapy dogs?
• How much do you charge for a pet puppy? What distinguishes a pet from a show puppy?
• May I have the puppy with natural ears?

Now you have the questions, but what are the right answers? Ideally the breeder you choose should have no fewer than five years in the breed, and more is better! Most of the top breeders of Minis in the United States have been "in" the breed for decades. It's not uncommon for Mini breeders to also breed Standard or Giant Schnauzers, but avoid any breeder who has a half dozen different breeds at his or her kennel (unless the breeder boards other dogs or handles show dogs professionally).

Every breeder has a reason for selecting a particular female to breed. A breeder who has a limited program may in fact own only two bitches, both of whom were selected for their good qualities. Soundness, a friendly temperament, good health, and overall excellent type are reasons for breeding a particular dam. The breeder may have selected the male dog because of his strong type, track record of producing sound puppies, his show record, or his pedigree. Although you may not be perfectly clear on every detail the breeder offers, it's more important that he or she has reasons for the mating. Obviously, you don't want the breeder to tell you that the sire was the only dog in the neighborhood that looked like a Miniature Schnauzer!

The breeder should acquire clearance from CERF or OFA for the sire and the dam as well as the pups, certifying that eyes are clear of cataracts and free of other hereditary concerns. It's always best for breeders to be honest about what problems they've encountered—even better if they tell prospective owners what steps they've taken to eliminate the problems from their breeding programs. Unfortunately, not all breeders feel this way and are afraid to admit to health issues in their lines. This only worsens matters for everyone.

Review the sales contract carefully and make sure that the breeder is willing to take the puppy back should you encounter a problem a few weeks down the road. Most breeders do not want their puppies abandoned and will gladly accept them back—no questions asked.

References! Talking to satisfied customers will be very helpful. Realistically, however, the breeder isn't going to give you a list of unhappy customers, but it's still worth the extra effort to make a couple of phone calls. You'd be amazed at how much you can learn from other Miniature Schnauzer owners.

Both sire and dam must be AKC-registered, and the breeder should register the litter as well. Puppy owners usually then register their puppies individually once they've selected the pups' names.

Not every breeder shows his or her own dogs, though many hire handlers to show their dogs or work with co-breeders and backers. Ideally, the show ring is the arena in which the quality of a breeder's stock is

assessed by judges. It may look like a beauty contest or an exhibition, but a dog show in fact serves a purpose. Only the best dogs—the ones chosen by the judges at dog shows—should be chosen as stock for breeding programs. When the best dogs are bred, the breed improves with each generation, with offspring resembling (or bettering) their parents and grandparents. Of course, it doesn't always work like that, but in a perfect world, it would.

A dog that is trained and certified for therapy work represents the ideal temperament for a companion dog. That a breeder's dogs are ideal candidates for therapy work can only mean that they make great family companions too.

Breeders should be direct with puppy buyers, especially when it concerns money. Agree on a price from the get-go. A breeder will indicate which puppies are available for pet homes. Even if you're willing to pay the show-puppy price, the breeder may not be willing to sell you that puppy. A breeder naturally wants his or her best puppies out in the show ring, winning ribbons and promoting the breeder's reputation. If you're interested in a show puppy, be prepared for not only the higher price but also the likelihood of having to show your dog and possibly agreeing to a future breeding.

If you want a puppy with natural ears, tell the breeder right away. Most breeders are willing to accommodate this request.

In addition to answering and asking questions, look for the following when visiting a breeder's home or kennel:
- the puppies are clean, active, and vibrant in appearance
- the surroundings are clean and smell good

Disarmed by a bevy of Mini puppies as cute as this one, a new owner would be facing a difficult decision. Rely on the breeder's insight into each pup's personality to help you make the best choice.

- the adult dogs on the premises are friendly and well cared for
- all of the dogs are Miniature Schnauzers (or perhaps Standards or Giants)
- the dam (mother) of the litter is friendly, healthy, and attentive to her puppies
- the breeder has a pleasant rapport with all of his or her dogs

Most breeders raise their puppies in their homes, though some well-established kennels may have auxiliary buildings where dogs are kept. You will know you are in the home of an accomplished breeder or full-fledged "dog person" when you see the walls lined with ribbons and champion certificates representing the achievements earned at dog shows.

THE PUPPIES IN PERSON

The next part of assessing the breeder is meeting the puppies. An active litter of baby Miniature Schnauzers can make any dog lover's heart skip a beat! Those floppy, folded ears and black button noses can seduce even the most discerning puppy buyer. However, you must look past the cuteness for signs of quality breeding and care.

It's not uncommon for the sire of the litter to not be on the premises, but you should always be able to meet the dam.

The puppies should be clean, relatively speaking—Minis are earthdogs who don't mind getting dirty, and young pups poop much faster than breeders can scoop. Even so, puppies should smell like puppies. They should be solid for their size, without extended bellies, and have clear eyes and noses. Watery discharge from noses, eyes, or ears is unwelcome, and none of the puppies should be coughing or snorting.

Always ask the breeder to see the dam (mom) of the litter. She should be on the premises because the pups are not weaned until around eight weeks of age. Your puppy will inherit the features of his parents, which means that the personality of the dam reflects your puppy's future. She should be friendly and approachable, though don't be surprised if she's a bit protective of her charges. She may also look scraggly compared to the pretty, groomed dogs in this book: that's what rearing, cleaning, feeding, and chasing a litter of puppies can do to a good dog!

Once you have settled upon a breeder, selecting the right puppy from the litter is your next hurdle. Rely on the breeder's advice about which puppy might best suit your lifestyle.

After spending so much time with the puppies, the breeder has the best sense of each individual puppy's personality. Sometimes one puppy stands out and instantly "chooses" you, but not always. A bouncy sextet of Mini puppies can confound an eager buyer. You may label one puppy as the boldest of the litter and another as the most reluctant from your initial observations, but the breeder should know each puppy's likes and dislikes, funny habits, and inclinations. Miniature Schnauzers are intelligent, sensitive creatures, so it's not as easy to predict personalities as it is coat texture or height.

An experienced breeder, who has bred many generations of his or her own line of Miniature Schnauzers, often can predict how each puppy will grow up in terms of size, coat, and type. Personalities tend to vary from dog to dog.

At a Glance ...

Once you decide upon the sex and color of your new Miniature Schnauzer puppy, you can begin your search for a puppy. The only way to find a great puppy is to find a great breeder.

· ·

Just as you need to know what qualifies a puppy as great—type, coat, friendliness, activity—you need to know what makes a breeder exceptional. Know what questions you should ask, and be ready to answer the breeder's questions head on. An experienced, knowledgeable breeder isn't shy about discussing health issues and screening with new buyers. The health of a litter is the top priority of a good breeder.

· ·

When you meet a litter of well-bred Mini puppies at the home of a great breeder, you will have no doubt that the research and time have paid off.

CHAPTER FOUR

Welcome Home, Mini

Bringing a puppy into your home is a big event, no matter how small the puppy. It's ideal if you can plan the homecoming for the beginning of a vacation week from work. Taking a few days off to acclimate the puppy and begin his training and socialization will pay off for the whole first year and beyond. You don't want to squeeze the puppy pickup in between dropping off your dry cleaning and running into the mall to

Day by Day

Set a consistent daily schedule for your puppy from the first day he arrives. Even if you don't lead a structured existence, make an effort to establish a routine for your dog. This will help you with housetraining, crate use, meals, and overall obedience. Don't worry if you have to tweak the schedule a bit as your puppy settles in, but try not to diverge from it entirely.

catch a one-day sale. You'll want to spend some time getting to know the puppy, introducing him to your family and close friends, and teaching him the basic house rules.

HAVE A PLAN

A new puppy requires a lot of planning to minimize the disruption to both of your lives. The more carefully you plan for the puppy's arrival, the smoother and more enjoyable his first days at home will be. Your own peace and sanity are at stake here, too, so make all of the important decisions and preparations prior to carrying your Mini baby through the front door.

- Where is the puppy going to sleep, and in what?
- Where will the puppy's feeding station be?
- In which rooms will the puppy be allowed?
- Where will the puppy spend his days?
- Where will the puppy do his business?
- Are the yard, garage, shed, and home puppy-proof (a.k.a. safe for the puppy)?
- What pet supplies do you need to purchase before the puppy comes home?
- Who will be the puppy's veterinarian?
- Which family member will be in charge of the puppy's feeding, training, and socialization?
- Is everyone in the family, other pets included, prepared for the new addition?

Sleeping is one of every puppy's favorite activities—behind playing, chewing, and eating, but still up there on the list. The puppy's sleeping location is essentially wherever you place his crate and dog bed. He should sleep near the family but out of the way of foot traffic and drafts. The puppy must feel warm and safe when he's in his special sleeping place.

Most dog owners feed their pets in the kitchen, but an adjoining room may work better for your own situation. It's advisable to put a placemat under the puppy's bowls to keep the floor from getting wet and soiled. Keep the mat clean and wipe the area underneath it every day with a pet-safe cleanser.

The puppy should not have an all-access pass to your living space. You need to keep a close eye on him when he's exploring the house. No matter how expertly you puppy-proof, your Mini will discover something you don't want him to. Closed doors and baby gates can keep your puppy out of off-limits areas. Be sure that everyone in the household knows where the puppy is and is not allowed, and be sure that he's always supervised whenever he's roaming free in the house.

If you have a backyard where your puppy can play and relieve himself, you must be certain that it's absolutely secure. A small puppy

can easily squeeze through or under a chain-link fence if the links are too wide or not embedded well into the ground. Board-on-board or solid fencing is safe, though not permitted in all communities.

The puppy should spend his days in his designated area and in his crate, an essential tool that will be at the top of your shopping list. He can earn more freedom as he gets older and learns to abide by the house rules, but in the beginning, limiting his space is important for both training and safety.

Puppies need more sleep than you might think. This youngster has drifted off in a laundry basket in the backyard.

We cannot over-emphasize the importance of the puppy's safety in and around your home. Simple everyday items and household products can harm or kill a puppy, so humans have to be quick and aware about keeping potential harmful items away from the Miniature Schnauzer (and the Miniature Schnauzer away from potential dangers). New parents these days are super-cautious about their babies' health and safety, and new puppy parents need to be equally on their toes, especially since a twelve-week-old puppy is a lot more mobile and adventurous than a like-aged baby.

We live in the age of the pet mega-store, and these terrific pet supermarkets are within driving distances of most people in the urban and suburban areas of the country. We are spoiled for choice, so some good

A PIECE OF HISTORY

The first Schnauzer registered by the AKC was Norwood Victor, a Standard, in 1904, the year the Standard Schnauzer was accepted. In 1926, the breed was renamed Schnauzer and was moved to the Terrier Group. The first Miniature Schnauzer registered with the AKC was Schnapp v Dornbusch of Hitofa. In 1927 the Schnauzer breed was split into two varieties, Miniature and Standard, and was reclassified as separate breeds in 1933.

The breed's first parent club, the Schnauzer Club of America (originally named the Wirehaired Pinscher Club), founded in 1925, fostered both the Standard and the Miniature Schnauzer, then considered one breed. The current club, the American Miniature Schnauzer Club (AMSC) was formed in 1933.

Once the puppy comes home, you'll be too busy to think about shopping and puppy-proofing the house. Be prepared before the happy day arrives.

shopping advice is warranted and is given later in this chapter.

You'll take the puppy to the vet's office for a preliminary checkup within the first few days of bringing the puppy home, so it's vital to select a vet prior to picking up the puppy. Your breeder, your dog-owning friends, or a local dog club can recommend good vets in your area. Be sure to schedule the appointment ahead of time for sometime during puppy's first week home; you want to be certain right off the bat that he is sound and healthy. Mention any concerns about the puppy's health and bring along whatever paperwork the breeder has provided. The vet will ask about how the puppy has been eating, drinking, and eliminating; check his heart, breathing, weight, and body temperature; take a look at his skin and coat condition; examine his ears, throat, mouth, gums, and teeth; and do a routine eye exam. Even though most breeders routinely deworm their pups, bring along a fecal sample so the vet can check for worms.

While it's important for the whole family to be involved in the puppy's upbringing, one person should be in charge of the puppy's training and care. Everyone in the household may be excited about a new puppy and be eager to walk him, feed him, and brush him, but enthusiasm for the daily routine often wanes as the puppy grows up. In truth, it's easier to care for a well-trained adult dog than it is a mischievous, unpredictable puppy. Good training and socialization from the beginning pay great dividends for years to come.

LITTLE PEOPLE, MEET LITTLE DOG

If there are young people in the family, especially children seven years old and younger, talk to them about how to act around a puppy before the pup comes home. Eight-week-old Miniature Schnauzers may look like fuzzy playthings, but they're living, sentient creatures. Proper behavior toward a new puppy begins with knowing how to greet a puppy (or any dog), which includes speaking in an "inside voice," moving slowly, offering the back of the hand for the puppy to sniff, and rubbing under the puppy's chin (not on top of his head). Instruct your children to not try to pick the puppy up—accidents can happen very easily, and a fall from just a couple of feet in the air can injure a small puppy. Simple mishaps can upset a puppy so deeply that he will mistrust handling by young people in the future.

The best way for children to interact with the puppy is to sit on the floor and call the puppy to them by clapping their hands and softly calling the puppy's name. Let the puppy explore each child's lap on his own. Explain to the younger children that the puppy needs a lot of sleep, just like a baby does, so that he can grow up and be strong and healthy. As the saying goes, let sleeping Minis lie.

SHOPPING CART

Seek the advice of your breeder before hitting the stores! He or she will be happy to give you some guidance about the products that he or she's had the most success with. An experienced Miniature Schnauzer person will know the best kind of collar and leash to start out with. The breeder will likely encourage you to continue feeding the same brand of food that the puppy's been eating and will suggest dietary changes as the puppy grows. Ask about crates, food and water vessels, brushes and combs, chew toys, and so forth. You will save money by choosing the right tools first: quality supplies can last the dog's lifetime.

You can also take advantage of the knowledge of the staff at any of the pet-supply stores close to your home. A well-run pet superstore or a good independent pet-supply shop owned by people who know dogs can be a valuable resource. You can browse a wide range of food, supplies, and specialty items, and an employee should be able to give you some advice about the merchandise.

Another great outlet for pet supplies is an AKC dog show. You should be able to find a show in your area because AKC events take place around the

Consider the Microchip

In addition to using a dog collar and ID tag, think about having your veterinarian insert a microchip in your dog to help find him if he ever gets lost. When scanned, the microchip will show your dog's unique microchip number so that your dog can be returned to you as soon as possible. Go to www.akc-car.org to learn more about the nonprofit American Kennel Club Companion Animal Recovery (AKC CAR) pet recovery system.

Since 1995, the AKC CAR service has been selected by millions of dog owners who are grateful for the peace of mind and service that AKC CAR offers.

AMERICAN KENNEL CLUB®

country every weekend of the year. Dog shows are great places to meet other Miniature Schnauzer lovers, and many of the big all-breed shows feature a carnival of trade stands that cater to every need of the modern dog owner.

Bowls

For the rough and tumble Miniature Schnauzer, stainless-steel bowls make the most sense. You're purchasing feeding vessels, not chew toys, and stainless-steel bowls are dishwasher safe, virtually indestructible, and fairly inexpensive. They can also endure the weather outdoors, so you can always have a water bowl on the patio.

Pet-supply stores offer many other kinds of bowls, too. Plastic, ceramic, and earthenware bowls may look more attractive, but they cannot be sanitized in the dishwasher the way stainless steel can be. Getting tip-proof bowls proves smart for owners of Mini pups who love to play and splash in their water.

Food

What good's a bowl without F-O-O-D? Your breeder should recommend the best brand of puppy food for you to start with. There's no such thing as good cheap dog food—you get what you pay for when it comes to kibble (and most other things in life). Be frugal in other areas—premium quality food pays off in good health, a shiny coat, energy, and much more. Unless you have a super-fussy puppy (which is not common with Miniature Schnauzers), you don't have to worry that your dog isn't going to like his food. Some owners think that because their dog eats his food with gusto that it must be a good-quality food, but dogs are like children and will eat what tastes good: most of the low-grade dog foods taste good thanks in part to sugar and chemical flavorings.

Collar and ID Tag

Begin your puppy with an adjustable buckle collar that you can expand as he grows. A lightweight nylon collar is preferred to a leather collar for the puppy. Keep an eye on the puppy's collar because his neck will widen notch by notch faster than you think.

A traditional identification tag attached to the puppy's collar should include your name, address, and phone number. In this age of GPS, it's no surprise that dog collars have taken advantage of such technology. You can purchase a high-tech dog collar with a built-in Global Positioning System that will alert you (via phone or email) whenever your dog has wandered outside his designated area.

Some puppies name themselves or at least give you clues about what name would be best. Be creative, but choose a name that rollos off your tongue naturally.

Naming Your Puppy

For years, dog books have been offering silly advice about naming your dog: don't select a name that rhymes with "no" or "sit," and don't choose a complicated name with more than three syllables. In naming your Miniature Schnauzer, you may be inclined to select a name based on the breed's heritage, such as Helga, Otto, or Ludwig, which would be fun for a German breed. Human names (such as Fred, Felix, and Sue) have become far more popular for dogs than the old doggy standbys such as Fido and Rover. Some owners like to name their dogs after their favorite celebrities, so it's not uncommon to meet Mini Schnauzers named Justin, Brad, Adele, and Brandy (which was once a popular dog name too!).

Select a name that feels right to you, one that is ear-catching and that captures the personality of your Mini. You will use the dog's name any time you praise the dog or call the dog to you, but avoid using the dog's name with corrections: you always want your Mini to associate his name with something happy and positive.

Leashes

Purchase an 8-foot nylon or cloth leash to attach to the collar for leash training, daily walks, and puppy kindergarten classes. Once the puppy is reliable on the conventional leash, you can purchase a good flexible lead, which is housed in a plastic handle and extends and retracts with the push of a button. The 16-foot length is designed for Miniature Schnauzers and other similarly sized dogs, allowing them more leeway to run and explore.

Gates and Pens

Useful, or even essential, for puppy-proofing some homes, doggy (or baby) gates can confine a puppy to a designated part of the house. Look for gates with bars that are spaced closely enough to prevent your puppy from squeezing through or getting a foot or jaw stuck between them.

If you have an open floor plan, you may not be able to utilize puppy gates, so you'll have to invest in an exercise pen (or "ex-pen"). An ex-pen is an expandable unit that stands on its own, can be sized to the area you require, and be used both indoors or outdoors. The most durable ex-pens are constructed of heavy-gauge wire that's coated with acrylic. The standard eight-panel pen ranges from 2 to 4 feet in height and allows the puppy plenty of space to play. A safe puppy pen can also be assembled with interlocking play-yard panels available at baby-supply stores.

Crate and Bedding

A hard plastic dog crate does double duty for your puppy: it serves as his sleeping quarters and his travel carrier. As the puppy learns to accept the crate as his "safe place," he will instinctively go to it for his naps and quiet time. Most importantly, the crate simplifies house-training tenfold because dogs naturally do not want to eliminate where they sleep (or eat). To reinforce the puppy's strong association with the crate, you can initially feed him his meals in the crate.

For bedding in the crate, start off with a couple of bath towels or a blanket for the puppy to lie on. Alternatively, you can purchase a crate pad, which is just as easy to launder. Keep your Mini's bedding clean and dry, and when the puppy has an accident in the crate, be prepared to disinfect it thoroughly with a dog-safe cleaning product.

You can also purchase a dog bed for your Mini to curl up on when he's outside his crate, hanging out with the family. Choose a simple, machine-washable bed; once the puppy is house-trained, you can splurge on something more elaborate and attractive. Avoid wicker beds because puppies and adults alike tend to chew on them, and sharp pieces of wicker can all too easily cause injuries or choking.

Grooming Tools

To keep your Miniature Schnauzer looking like a Miniature Schnauzer, a certain amount of grooming is involved. The dog's coat consists of a smooth undercoat and a hard, wiry outer coat. The only way to maintain the desired hard texture of the outer coat is by hand plucking, the preferred method of show groomers. Most pet Minis have their coats clippered, which maintains the outline of the coat but alters the texture. Here's a list of grooming supplies you'll need to purchase for your Mini:

Brushes and combs: The Miniature Schnauzer's coat requires a slicker brush (short metal pins angled at the ends). A metal Greyhound comb, which has both closely spaced and medium-spaced teeth, is the comb of choice for Mini groomers.

Nail clippers: Most owners find that the guillotine-type nail clippers are the easiest to use.

Scissors and shears: If you plan to trim your Mini's coat yourself, invest in a good-quality pair of scissors and a pair of single-blade thinning shears (42 to 46 teeth) to blend the coat between the scissored and clippered areas.

Electric clippers: To clipper your Mini's coat at home, you'll need a top-quality clipper with detachable blades; the AMSC recommends the

Young puppies are ready for anything. Have a plan to socialize and train your puppy so that he is assured that you are the human in charge.

Never underestimate a tiny puppy's potential for mischief. The cuteness is merely a distraction from the Mini's intentions to wreak havoc on your home and life!

Oster A5 and the Andis AG. You will use the #10, #30, and #40 blades, and maybe a size 7F (full tooth) and #15 as well. The higher-numbered blades cut closer, so the #40 blade, for instance, is used to clipper the ears, while the #10 blade is usually used on the body. Read the instructions that come with the clipper and seek the guidance of an experienced groomer or Miniature Schnauzer owner.

Grooming table: The Mini requires regular grooming, so if you're going to save money by doing it yourself, you'll want to save your back by purchasing a grooming table. A table that has an arm with a noose extension is handy to keep the dog in place. The table should have a rubber nonskid surface so that the dog feels safe when he's in position.

PUPPY-PROOFING THE HOUSE

After all of the preparation and forethought you've invested into your new Miniature Schnauzer, the puppy's safety in your house and yard is paramount. It's a puppy's nature to find mischief, and he will follow his little black nose to the corners of the universe. When puppy-proofing, think outside the box. Get down on all fours and look around. The undersides of furniture, the crevices between and behind appliances, and miles of computer cords and electrical wires are much more noticeable when you're 12 inches off the floor (like your puppy is). You'll also learn how thorough your house-cleaning skills are when your puppy unearths a tumbleweed of dust from under the bed or behind the sofa.

Let's do a sweep through the whole house, room by room, and identify potential concerns. Starting in the bathroom, lower the toilet seat and make the trash can inaccessible (such as by latching the lid or raising it from the floor). Be sure the puppy can't open under-the-sink cabinets or linen closets where he could find medicine bottles, dental floss, toilet bowl cleaners, and other items that could be harmful to him. The puppy may delight in unspooling your bathroom tissue or pulling a washcloth from the side of the tub, but these will likely not harm him...unless he swallows them.

On to the bedroom, which can also present potential hazards. It's time to heed your parents' instructions and pick up your clothes. Puppies love the smell of dirty clothes (they smell like their favorite humans times ten). The mystery of the missing sock is solved when there's a puppy in the house. Your Mini will love to retrieve your socks and undergarments from under the bed or the floor. Be sure to put them in the hamper. Secure electrical wires away from the puppy's reach, and keep ashtrays where the puppy cannot get to them—eating a handful of cigarette butts is even worse than secondhand smoke.

The kitchen is the most alluring—yet the worst—room in the house. Keep your cleaning supplies, including mops and buckets, out of the puppy's reach. Again, secure electrical cords that might be dangling from countertops or on the floor. Fasten kitchen cabinets with safety stoppers (the same kind used for children's safety). The kitchen garbage can is a temptation all its own, so it must be kept in a secure cabinet or behind a door. Puppies love to revisit yesterday's dinner scraps and find out what other great stuff you foolishly discarded.

The rule with garages and sheds is to keep the puppy out of them because there are too many lethal agents and potential disasters to list. Your puppy can die from ingesting rat poisons, insect-control products, antifreeze, gasoline, plant fertilizers, certain types of mulch, and other backyard chemicals. Sharp tools and heavy equipment further make the garage and shed a danger zone to avoid at all times.

HONEY, WE'RE HOME!!

The day has finally come. You've picked up the puppy and all of the important paperwork from the breeder, and you've arrived home. Immediately upon getting out of the car, carry the puppy into the backyard or to whatever outdoor area he'll use to do his business. When the puppy piddles or poos, give him lots of praise and a rub on the chin.

If the yard is fenced, let the puppy sniff around off lead after he eliminates. Follow the puppy to make sure he's not getting into trouble, encourage him to play with a new toy, and speak to him softly and positively. Don't get carried away—you're trying to keep the excitement to a minimum. While the puppy is investigating the backyard, invite other

Fun Playthings

Most pet-supply superstores are like "Dog Toys 'R' Us," and you will be overwhelmed by the selection. Leave your Santa-sized bag at home and begin by purchasing just two or three items. There are plenty of great dog toys made of rubber, nylon, plastic, cloth, and so forth. Start by selecting a soft toy, such as a nice fat stuffed rodent with a squeaker inside, to get your Mini's terrier instincts excited. A properly sized sturdy nylon bone is another good choice, as is a rubber ball or tennis ball. Safety is more important than fun, so select wisely and always supervise the puppy when he has a new toy. Avoid any toys that look flimsy or with parts that can be removed by puppy teeth.

The Ride Home

members of your household to come out and meet the puppy.

Once everyone has said hello and the puppy has done his business, you can pick him up and bring him inside the house to his area. Escort the puppy around as he explores. Depending on the time of year, the change in temperature may give the puppy the urge to piddle again. Carefully watch the puppy and be ready to whisk him away to his outside area. If he starts to sniff around or circle, pick him up and take him back outside right away. With an eight-week-old puppy, there's only a few seconds between "the sign" and the "the puddle." Be patient and remember that a puppy this young has the same bladder control as a human infant, which is to say none. Giving the puppy lots of praise every time he relieves himself outdoors is laying the groundwork for future housebreaking success.

A young puppy will likely be eating three times a day, so when it's lunchtime, offer the puppy a meal (the same food the breeder recommended). After he eats, take the pup outside again to eliminate; the digestion process will take less than an hour, sometimes just twenty or thirty minutes. Now it's time for a little siesta: remove the puppy's collar and place him in his crate with a soft stuffed toy so he can enjoy a nap. Close the crate door and leave the room so he can settle down. Do not put food or water in the crate because this will only invite accidents and messes.

The puppy may fuss for a few minutes—ignore him and go do some laundry. Do not remove him from the crate because he's whining; if you let him out, you're teaching him that whining equals winning. Tell the puppy he's a good dog and comfort him with a soft voice. He should soon fall asleep. Once he awakens from his nap, let him out of his crate and get him right outside to urinate, being sure to tell him he's a good boy.

Later in the afternoon or early evening, offer your puppy a treat. Hold it out to him in your hand and let him sniff it, and then use the treat to lure him over to the crate. Toss the treat into the crate and encourage the puppy to retrieve it. Once he's in the crate, tell him how smart he is and toss him another treat. You are trying to convince him that good things happen in his crate. There's nothing scary about the crate: he doesn't associate the metal bars with the state penitentiary like humans do!

After the puppy eats his dinner, take him outside again and then remove his water for the night. When night falls and bedtime calls, take the puppy out one last time and then place him in his crate. Most owners like to place the crate in their bedroom so that the puppy can see, hear, and smell them. If you have the self-control and patience to resist caving in to the puppy's whimpering and crying, then share your bedroom. If you think you don't, you're better off placing the puppy in another room so you'll have less temptation to "free him from his cage." A night-light on in the room often helps to reduce puppy anxiety, as does some soft music or talk radio.

Check in on the puppy. If he's making noise for attention, don't fret and don't give in. If you let the puppy know that he can control you by

whining, he's on his way to becoming a spoiled kid. Of course, if the puppy is restless in his crate, you may have to take him to his outside place for a quick wee. This is a no-frills middle-of-the-night business trip—no treats, toys, or nonsense. Have your robe, jacket, and sneakers ready, because it's not uncommon for young puppies to need to go once during the night. Your puppy should not keep you up all night, but your sleep may be interrupted during the puppy's first week.

At a Glance ...

Before the homecoming day arrives, be sure you have a plan for your life with a puppy, including supplies, food, safety around your home and yard, house rules, a veterinarian's services, and so forth.

. . . .

Be a smart shopper when stocking your house for the puppy. Purchase the best equipment that you can afford, and you'll save money in the long run.

. . . .

When the puppy comes home, be prepared to focus completely on the puppy for his first day and night in the house. He'll adjust to your schedule with little difficulty, but be patient and nurturing. Everyone in the family should be ready to welcome the puppy, though children require supervision whenever they're around young puppies. Introduce them carefully and be aware that a child can injure a puppy very easily.

CHAPTER FIVE

Your Mannerly Mini

Not everyone is a born boss. Some folks are happy to follow the bossy ones and not stray from the course. A survey of Miniature Schnauzers, however, undoubtedly would reveal that most think they're boss material and imagine their intelligence to exceed that of their human caregivers. For generations, Mini owners have described their dogs as having "near-human brains," which both simplifies and complicates training.

BE THE ONE WITH THE ANSWERS

Dog training is essentially a human's ability to convey to the dog what the human expects of the dog. Minis are excellent judges of character, and they effortlessly can see through a phony. As the human in the relationship, it's vital that you know what you consider acceptable and unacceptable in terms of your dog's behavior. Nothing is black and white (or pepper and salt) when it comes to determining what's right and wrong; for example, it's not that sitting on the white satin settee is *wrong*, it's just that you don't allow it.

From day one, you have to be able to demonstrate to your Mini that you have *the* answer to every question. You are omniscient, the all-knowing owner. Dogs get nervous when they think that their owners are floundering, and Minis have particularly little patience for mediocrity. If you're to be the boss—and you must be—then you have be decisive, informed, and convincing.

Omniscience, in and of itself, isn't enough to persuade a Miniature Schnauzer. The human-animal bond that we hear so much about is entirely composed of trust. You earn your Mini's trust by showing him that you are competent, consistent, and considerate. Your unshakeable leadership role is also built on goodwill and good treats, which is why positive-training (reward-based) methods are the best way to earn a dog's trust. Punishment and physical correction only serve to damage the developing trust between a dog and his owner.

YES AND NO

Positive training doesn't mean always saying "yes." In fact, teaching the meaning of "no" is critical to your Miniature Schnauzer's understanding and acceptance of the household rules. Dogs perceive themselves as

It's the owner's responsibility to train his or her dog. When you have a dog as bright as the Mini, you better bring your "A game" or you'll be the one learning lessons.

pack animals, which means they need not only a leader but also structure. Pack animals are programmed to abide by a set of social rules, and you just need to provide and enforce the rules.

The tone of voice you use for "no" should be different than the tone of voice you use for every other word or command. It's the one word that will stop your dog in his tracks and force him to reconsider what he's doing at the moment. If you don't use an authoritative, stern voice, you'll find yourself repeating "no" constantly—and the effectiveness of the word diminishes every time you repeat it. If the puppy doesn't think you mean it *every* time you say it, he will test you to see what he can get away with if he wrinkles his irresistible little 'stache and flashes a smile at you.

Whenever you catch your puppy in a moment of wrongdoing, you must stop him by telling him "no" in a serious, "I-mean-business" tone. Remember, Minis respect authority and confidence.

WALKING ON A LEASH

Introduce your Miniature Schnauzer to his lightweight buckle collar or harness and his lead by twelve weeks of age. Initial lessons may consist of nothing more than familiarizing your pup with the sensation of wearing this equipment. Once he has learned to accept the collar or harness, begin attaching the lead. Either let him drag it around the floor or hold it and let him walk wherever he wants to. Don't skimp on the praise and encouragement, and never, ever pull or drag him along on the lead.

Some puppies are ready to go exploring as soon as you put the lead on them, but others may take quite a bit longer. If your pup is unsure, you will just have to be patient and keep coaxing him with toys, treats, and praise until he feels confident enough to walk with you. Do not reprimand him or act frustrated! Under no circumstances should you do anything to create a negative perception about the process.

Keep the lessons short and don't subject your Mini to busy streets or parks during this training. Learning to accept the lead and walk with you, all while ignoring distractions, can be quite a lot for a puppy to assimilate at one time. If you don't have a quiet backyard, hold your lessons indoors. Give the pup a few days to get the hang of it.

If you are dealing with a really tough customer who absolutely refuses to walk on lead, try enlisting the help of a friend with an older, well-trained dog. Most puppies will overcome their reluctance when they see that other dogs enjoy walking on lead.

Once your puppy is walking reliably, begin teaching him to heel at your side before he has the opportunity to form bad habits. This is especially important if you plan to show your Mini in conformation or obedience, but that's not the only reason—a wildly lunging dog is a nuisance to pedestrians, and he can put himself in serious danger with such antics.

Heeling means that the puppy walks at your side and maintains your pace on a loose lead. Traditionally, dogs are taught to walk on the left side, but either side is fine—just pick one and stick with it. You can easily

How Does Your Garden Grow?

If you're an avid gardener with a yard full of beautiful flowers and foliage, you're wise to protect your plants and your earthdog from one another. Many commonly found plants have toxic properties when ingested by dogs, causing reactions ranging from mouth irritation and upset stomachs to organ failure and death. Here's a partial list of popular plants to avoid in your yard and home:

Aloe	Hydrangea	Peace lily
Amaryllis	Ivy	Philodendron
American holly	Lantana	Rhododendron
Autumn crocus	Lilly-of-the-valley	Rosary pea
Azalea	bush	Tulip
China berry	Meadow saffron	Verbena shrub
Christmas rose	Mistletoe	Yesterday, today
Daffodil	Morning glory	and tomorrow
Elephant's ear	Nightshade and	Yew and Japanese
Foxglove	deadly nightshade	Yew
Gladiolus	Oleander and yel-	
Hyacinth	low oleander	

trip over or step on a small dog who's constantly weaving back and forth. Keep treats in your hand or pocket on the side on which you're teaching the puppy to walk, using them to hold his attention and reward him for keeping pace. Use the command "heel" and verbal encouragement to get him moving if he slows down, stops, or pulls ahead; praise him and give him a treat when he returns to your side. Yanking on the lead can be counterproductive because many dogs instinctively respond by pulling even harder. Tugging on the leash can also potentially damage a young Mini's delicate neck.

THE HOUSE RULES

Even if you're not a "planner" by nature, you're going to have to transform yourself for the sake of your Miniature Schnauzer. Minis, like all dogs, prefer to be on a schedule. Canines are creatures of habit who thrive on routine. That's not to say that dogs don't get bored by repetition, but they do like to know what to expect. Dogs aren't up for surprises.

Structure begins with rules, and you and all members of your household need to agree on the house rules before your Mini comes home. The family should discuss and decide on the following:

- Will the puppy be permitted on the furniture?
- Is roughhousing and tug-of-war acceptable?
- Is the puppy allowed on the bed?
- Should upstairs or certain rooms be off-limits?
- Is the puppy allowed to bark when people come to the door?
- Which door will we use when we take the dog out?
- When is it okay to release the puppy from his crate?
- When should a person give the puppy a treat, and how many treats is too many?
- Should the puppy be allowed to jump up on people?

As you're teaching your Miniature Schnauzer manners, you'll see that all of these questions address relevant concerns. It only serves to confuse the puppy when the rules aren't enforced by everyone in the home. When certain members of the family permit the puppy to jump on them or to beg at the table, and others do not, the puppy doesn't comprehend what's expected of him and how he should behave. Consistency is one of the keys to training success.

THE POSITIVE POWER OF CHEESE

Food rewards work well when teaching obedience commands and for reinforcing good behavior related to house-training, such as sitting quietly in the crate and doing his business outdoors. Treats show the puppy that he's doing something that pleases you. Bribery is not a crime in the dog world, and dogs don't look down at bribes—they look forward to a taste

Set the Tempo

If your puppy lags behind or stops while you're out on a walk, make him catch up to you for a treat. If he pulls ahead or lunges, maintain your pace and make him come back to your side to get the treat. Suddenly reversing directions and then offering a treat is a helpful trick. He will soon learn that paying attention to your walking pace is worthwhile. And don't forget to praise him when he is walking politely on lead at the proper speed.

of liver for doing what their owners ask of them. The dog's brain may not comprehend why he should sit six times in a row or to stay in a submissive (down) position, but his stomach will be happy to comply.

Once the dog expects the treat, you can start to mix it up so that you're less predictable; for example, offer a treat for every third correct response and give verbal praise the rest of the time. You don't want the puppy to simply anticipate the desired response without listening to the actual command. Your puppy might sit instantly the minute he sees (or, more likely, smells) a treat in your hand, but you've given the down command instead. It's critical for the puppy to pay attention to you and not take the treat for granted. That way, his focus is sharper, and he's a more responsive student.

SOCIAL NETWORKING

Is your Mini a "people person"? Well-socialized dogs enjoy the company of people and other dogs. They are calm and confident when meeting new people, visiting new places, and encountering other dogs. The key ingredients for socialization are trust and love. Your puppy has to learn to trust you and to feel your sincere affection for him so that he can trust other people.

Exposing the young puppy to different people and places paves the way to socialization. If you're lucky enough to have acquired your Minia-

Make Your Puppy a S.T.A.R.

The American Kennel Club has a great program for new puppy owners called the S.T.A.R. Puppy® Program, which is dedicated to rewarding puppies that get off to a good start by completing a basic training class. S.T.A.R. stands for Socialization, Training, Activity, and Responsibility.

You must enroll in a six-week puppy-training course with an AKC-approved evaluator. When the class is finished, the evaluator will test your puppy on all of the training taught during the course, such as being free of aggression toward people and other puppies in the class, tolerating a collar or body harness, allowing his owner to take away a treat or toy, and sitting and coming on command.

If your puppy passes the test, he will receive a certificate and a medal. You and your puppy will also be listed in the AKC S.T.A.R. Puppy records. To learn more about the AKC S.T.A.R. Puppy Program or to find an approved evaluator, check out www.akc.org/puppies/training/index.cfm.

ture Schnauzer puppy from a good breeder who raised his or her litter in the home, you have a definite advantage. Puppies who are familiar with everyday noises, such as those from dishwashers, coffee grinders, TVs, washers and dryers, and vacuum cleaners, acclimate easier to their new homes. If you find that your puppy is alarmed by the normal sounds of your home, you will have to be conscious of this and demonstrate for him that none of these electrical "monsters" is scary.

Treats and positive reinforcement go a long way in convincing the puppy that the dishwasher or gas fireplace is not a threat. For example, after you offer the puppy his morning meal or a fun chew toy, turn on the dishwasher or coffeemaker so he's doing something he enjoys while listening to the sounds. Alternatively, you can call the puppy over to the running appliance and offer him a treat when he gets there. Treats help erase fear!

The first three months in your home are the most critical; canine behaviorists believe that puppies are most impressionable during their first twenty weeks of life. Once your Miniature Schnauzer is acclimated to his home environment, you should begin taking him out and about. Begin by walking the puppy around your neighborhood and allowing people to say hello to him. When someone approaches, ask him or her to kneel down and offer a hand to the puppy to sniff.

Progress to taking the puppy with you on your daily errands a few times each week. Think of dog-friendly places nearby, including the pet-supply store, a friend's or co-worker's home, a park, the beach, or an outdoor café.

It's important to keep all socialization experiences positive; for example, don't visit the local dog park at the busiest time of day, and avoid introducing your pup to a group of noisy children who could overwhelm him. Instead, start your Mini's acquaintance with other dogs and young people by visiting a friend with a well-behaved dog and equally polite children.

Frequent encounters with youngsters reinforce the puppy's confidence. Naturally, you must carefully supervise meetings with all children because they may be overly enthusiastic or unintentionally rough with a small puppy. There's nothing to gain from spending time with children who grab at or tease your puppy. All kids you meet should be instructed how to behave around a puppy so as not to upset or hurt the pup.

PUPPY CLASS

Puppy kindergarten classes offer great opportunities for your Miniature Schnauzer to meet other puppies in a controlled environment. The purpose of puppy classes is to teach basic manners, and you may find that you learn as much as your puppy does. These classes are usually avail-

Reward Good Behavior

Laying down the household laws and discouraging unwanted behaviors are important foundations for training, but rewards communicate instantly with the puppy. Humans naturally want to say "no" when a puppy is misbehaving, but they often forget to say "good dog" when the puppy is doing something right. Reinforcing positive behavior means that you give a puppy a treat for sitting nicely during grooming or for waiting before a door or gate is opened. You want to reinforce the simple everyday things, not just sit and stay. You don't need to provide a piece of cheese every time; verbal praise and a rub on the chin also relay your approval effectively.

able to pups as young as eight to ten weeks of age. It's a great investment of your time, and it gives you structured time for the puppy among your other everyday commitments. Enrolling in a puppy class guarantees that you'll spend quality time with your little one, which is so critical during his first twenty weeks of life.

Simple games and lessons taught to a puppy lay the foundation for his future canine education, leading to the AKC S.T.A.R. Puppy® Program and the AKC Canine Good Citizen® Program. The most important part of puppy kindergarten is fun with other puppies and people...you'll both be having fun and making new friends in no time.

READ YOUR PUPPY'S MIND

Knowing what your puppy is thinking when he's looking at you during training sessions is the key to teaching a smart dog like a Miniature Schnauzer. We hope this will be a review of the concepts you need to understand about dog training and behavior.

"I need to trust you 24/7." Every good relationship revolves around this five-letter word: T-R-U-S-T. A Miniature Schnauzer only obeys you because he believes that you are completely honest and trustworthy.

"I don't speak English, so don't try to impress me with lots of words." You will succeed faster by using simple one-word commands to teach basic behaviors. "Sit" will get results more quickly than "Be a good boy and sit down." Likewise, say "Stay" instead of "Stay right where you are." Be consistent about which words you use for which desired behaviors.

"Watch your tone of voice!" You know that the puppy's vocabulary is limited at best, but it's how you say it that really matters. When you want the dog to obey a command, you must speak authoritatively. Save your happy voice for offering treats and hugs.

"I heard you the first time." Don't repeat commands over and over and over. Say it once with conviction and mean it.

"I'm good...*very* good." Puppies live for praise and want to know when they're pleasing you. Use treats judiciously so that they make an impact when you offer them.

"Don't take your bad day out on me." Be consistent with your expectations every day. Don't allow your puppy up on the couch one day and then scold him for it the next day just because you're in a bad mood. Inconsistency only confuses dogs. In fact, if you're in foul spirits, it's better to just skip the training sessions that day.

"Oh, you mean *this* puddle." If you don't catch the puppy in the act, you cannot correct him. The puppy has to be standing in his puddle or with one foot in your dug-up daffodils for him to comprehend that he's done something wrong. You cannot correct a puppy for something he did at lunchtime when you come home at dinnertime.

"You're not my mother!" You should never hit your dog. Physical corrections can ruin your training efforts. The moment you raise a hand to your dog, he loses trust in you, and you're back to square one.

Will your Mini be allowed on the furniture? Before the puppy comes home, set the house rules and make sure that everyone in your household abides by them.

"Stop, you're boring me!" Keep training sessions interesting for little minds. Mix it up, keep it fresh, and always end on a positive note (reviewing a command that puppy does well and rewarding him for it).

"Thank you, but I don't like surprises." Canines are the proverbial creatures of habit, and they thrive on structure. Dogs like to know what to expect, so when you provide the structure and consistency that your puppy needs, you let him know that you can handle your role as leader with ease.

At a Glance ...

Miniature Schnauzers have convinced their owners that their dogs are the smartest on the planet. Training a dog as smart as the Mini requires an owner who is consistent, fair, and generally smarter than his/her dog. Know the correct response to every command and behavior before your Mini trains you first.

Manners begin at home, and walking a young Mini on his leash around the block will take lots of praise and practice. Consistency and structure are key to enforcing the house rules and establishing a puppy-training regimen. Inconsistent dog owners have ill-behaved pets.

Don't be afraid to bribe your dog to get the right response. A delicious smelly treat will yield better results than a formal lesson with a professional trainer. Enter your puppy in a puppy class and the AKC S.T.A.R. Puppy Program to reinforce your home lessons.

Begin socializing your puppy from the day he arrives to your home. Accustom the puppy to everyday household and outdoor noises. Bolster his bravery and his bravura with lots and lots of praise. Verbal fertilizer will make your Mini bloom into a happy, outgoing companion.

CHAPTER SIX

House-Training the Mini

Expectations abound when it comes to house-training the puppy. The goal in house-training is to relay your expectations to the puppy as directly as possible, keeping in mind that a young puppy has physical limitations. An adult dog can hold his urine for eight hours, but a puppy cannot. An owner's expectations for house-training are clear: do not relieve yourself inside the house. Unlike with other

aspects of training, though, communicating this to the puppy requires more than a simple one-word command.

Let's talk about the obvious accident-prone moments first. The puppy will have to relieve himself:

- After he eats and/or drinks
- Before you place him in the crate for down time
- Any time he wakes up from a nap
- Any time you release him from his crate
- First thing in the morning
- Before putting him to bed for the night

So far, that's about a dozen times each day when you know you'll need to get the puppy outside. With a young puppy, there are likely to be *another* dozen times when he'll need to relieve himself, times that are less predictable. A good rule of thumb is to get the puppy outside within three to five minutes after meals, drinks, naps or crate time, but you must keep a close eye on the puppy at all times and know that he could piddle at virtually any moment. A young puppy will give you very little indication that he has to go. As the puppy gets older, his signals become clearer.

CLEANLINESS IS NEXT TO DOGLINESS

Minis are naturally clean dogs and can be completely house-trained in a couple of months. Every dog, of course, learns at his own pace.

No matter how hard we try to predict the next Mayan apocalypse or take a stab at the winning Powerball numbers, we cannot see into the future. As the saying kind of goes, poo happens, and when it does, we have to clean it up. Finding droppings or puddles in the house is the least fun

Paper First

Paper-training for some dog owners is a transitional stage to outdoor training. Once the puppy's bodily control improves, you'll be able to make it outside in time when you see the puppy signaling. To begin paper-training, you'll choose a specific potty spot for the puppy indoors, where you'll lay down layers of newspaper or an absorbent puppy pad (designed for this purpose).

part of owning a dog, but it's an inevitable part of puppyhood, just as changing diapers is a part of babyhood.

Cleaning up the puppy's mess properly guarantees that he will not return to that spot to relieve himself. If you use basic household soap and water, you won't be able to detect traces of the accident, but your Miniature Schnauzer will—think about how much more powerful your dog's nose is compared to your own. That lingering odor will remind and tempt your puppy to use that spot again. Instead, choose a dog-safe organic disinfectant with an odor neutralizer to remove the smell

A PIECE OF HISTORY

Miniature Schnauzers in America began at the Marienhof Kennels of Marie Slattery, who was the first to import the breed from Germany beginning in 1924. Marienhof was active in the breed for half a century and produced over one hundred champions.

Many trainers like to use a relief command, a signal that the puppy should attend to his business. "Go potty" is the most obvious, but you can be creative or use whatever word you're comfortable with (not everyone likes to say "poo"). Minis are alert little dogs, so try to limit the distractions when you take your dog out to eliminate. Keep the chatter to a minimum (don't be on your cell phone) and don't putter around the yard while he's sniffing and thinking about going.

completely. Pet stores offer a few different brands that are designed for the specific purpose of removing pet odors. Don't use harsh household cleaners that contain bleach or ammonia. These are too strong for use around dogs—remember that powerful canine nose and imagine the smell of ammonia times 50,000!

INDOOR AND OUTDOOR TRAINING

The idea that your Mini Schnauzer's powerful canine nose can sniff out where he's relieved himself previously is what we count on to train the puppy to eliminate in the *desired* spot—which is not smack in the middle of your kitchen floor or behind a potted plant in the family room.

Begin by selecting a spot where your Mini should relieve himself, whether it be grass, gravel, or pavement. The dog must know where the designated place is and have access to it. He will learn to signal to you by heading for the door that leads outdoors to his spot.

Miniature Schnauzers are popular dogs for city dwellers, and house-training (or apartment-training) presents specific challenges to urban dog owners. If you are attempting to train a young puppy on the tenth floor of a downtown building, you're likely to start by paper-training. The chances of a young puppy's "holding it" during an elevator ride or trip down several flights of stairs are remote.

With a puppy up to twelve weeks old, you can count on his needing to relieve himself once an hour (while he's awake). At around the three-month mark, puppies have more control of their bladders and bowels but still will need to go out once every two hours (or about eight times) between morning and nighttime. At around five months of age, the pup-

py is reliable with five or six trips a day, and adults usually are fine with three or four. This varies from dog to dog, regardless of breed.

Your house-training schedule starts first thing in the morning. As soon as your Mini wakes up, take him to his designated area. Once he piddles, you can say "good morning" (and "good dog!") and start your day. Within ten minutes of the puppy's finishing his breakfast, take him to his spot again. Make sure he does what he is there for, and immediately reward him with praise and a treat when he does.

When you take him to his spot, give him ten or so minutes to do his thing. Don't make the mistake of giving up after three minutes and taking him back inside, only to witness him peeing on the kitchen floor. Do your best to mask your impatience or annoyance: dogs pick up on our moods, and you don't want your Mini to think he's doing anything wrong during his pre-poo or pre-piddle ritual. If your puppy doesn't go, even after sufficient time outside, confine him to his crate for half an hour and then try again.

Every time your young Mini relieves himself, make a big fuss and tell him what a good dog he is. Don't overthink this: it's not that strange for the puppy to see his owner dancing around because the puppy emptied his bladder…well, no stranger than what a toddler thinks when he's sitting on the toilet for the first time. Humans have high expectations when it comes to relief habits.

Your puppy's crate, puppy gates, and/or exercise pen come in handy to contain the puppy in the desired area of the house. Don't give him too much freedom too soon. Your Mini does not need free run of the house until he is completely trustworthy. Until that time, you must supervise him constantly, and it's easier to watch him when he's in a specific area where he's safe. Limit his space, and you'll limit the challenge of housebreaking.

The puppy's area in the house should include direct access to the outside door or his newspapers. Common sense is your guide here: your Miniature Schnauzer puppy can't be expected to signal at the back door if he's gated in a room on the second floor of your house or condo.

Accidents will happen; be prepared. You can only reprimand him for piddling in the house if he's in mid-piddle. Reprimanding a puppy after the fact is pointless—he will understand by your tone of voice that you are unhappy with him, but he won't connect the crime with the punishment.

Saying "no" (in a serious, low voice) while the puppy's peeing will not stop him midstream, but it will tell him that something is wrong. Once he finishes, scoop him up and carry him to his spot outdoors or the papers, and then say "good dog."

Don't sacrifice your puppy's trust to blow off

Don't Baby Him

steam when you find a puddle. There's no use crying over spilled anything. Just clean it up, get on with your day, and be sure to supervise your pup extra closely.

THE CRATE BEYOND

You'll find that experienced dog owners sing endless praises about the dog crate. It's sometimes hard for new owners to comprehend crate training, but don't overthink it. The puppy isn't a criminal, and he doesn't view the crate as "solitary confinement." You set the tone for the crate, introducing it to the puppy as a safe and relaxing place to hang out. You offer good things such as his meals and treats in the crate. They don't serve Happy Meals in prison!

From a house-training point of view, using a crate speeds up the process by days (actually weeks). The basic concept of crate training is that dogs don't like to relieve themselves where they sleep. A puppy's mother teaches him not to soil in their nest, and this natural aversion to soiling in the den encourages the puppy to "hold it." As long as you don't misuse

Crate training has lasting positive effects on a dog. The structure and discipline that the crate instills into the puppy's world pay off in good behavior further down the road.

the crate by leaving the puppy in it for hours on end, the crate works. Puppies can begin crate training by around four or five weeks of age, so if you're lucky, you acquired your Miniature Schnauzer from a breeder who introduced the litter to crates prior to the pups' being released to homes.

On the day you bring your puppy home, introduce him to the crate as part of his home environment. The crate should be positioned in the puppy's area, with the door open and a clean towel inside. He likely will walk into the crate to explore and may even curl up on the towel for a quick nap.

While many owners of large dogs get rid of their crates once housetraining is complete, the Mini Schnauzer owner can use it throughout his or her pet's life as a way to transport the dog in the car to appointments or shows, as a place for him to take his naps, as a safe haven when you need to keep him from being underfoot of guests or other visitors, and as a means of confinement when he is recovering from surgery or an illness. When used properly, the crate reinforces a dog's natural instinct for a safe den, and he will quickly learn to accept and love it.

Don't purchase an overly large crate. A medium-size crate is all you need for the puppy or adult Mini. It should be just roomy enough for the puppy to stand and turn around. If the crate is too big, the puppy may take to relieving himself in the corner of the crate where he's not sleeping, which is the beginning of a bad habit.

It usually takes a Miniature Schnauzer a few months to get the knack of housetraining, and most Mini owners report that their puppies are reliable by five months of age.

Always bring the puppy to the same spot in the yard to do his business.

At a Glance ...

Be proactive in house-training your Mini puppy: be three steps ahead of his next piddle, and never step backward without looking first. Puppies can piddle more than a dozen times a day!

. . . .

Dogs naturally don't want to soil their sleeping areas, hence owners and breeders have been successfully using crates to teach young puppies the essentials of house-training.

. . . .

Clean up every accident thoroughly, or your Mini will revisit and rewet or resoil the same spot over and over again.

. . . .

Be consistent in everything you do. The tighter your ship, the cleaner it will be. Take the pup to the same spot to relieve himself every time; carry the puppy outside every time you release him from his crate; keep a nearly constant eye on the puppy whenever he's exploring around the house.

CHAPTER SEVEN

The Teacher Is In!

Responsible dog owners train their dogs, regardless of whether their choice of breed is a tiny Yorkshire Terrier or a powerful guard dog like a German Shepherd. Any dog can become a problem if it is not properly trained, and the Miniature Schnauzer is no exception. Minis are exceptionally bright, which makes training them rewarding and a little challenging. Smart dogs are more demanding and bore

ABC's of Positive Training

The ABC's of positive training have been summarized like this: "A" is for Antecedent (what happened just prior to the behavior, usually what "triggered" the behavior), "B" is for Behavior (anything the dog does), and "C" is for Consequences (what comes right after the behavior). You shape "B" by controlling "A" and "C."

As you begin training, a command, such as sit or stay, is an antecedent (the moment before the behavior). You teach the dog to understand that the consequence of a behavior can be positive (either a reward or the promise of a treat), in which case the behavior that immediately preceded the reinforcement (sitting or staying) will tend to increase or be repeated. By withholding a treat or saying "no," the consequence is negative, intended to decrease the behavior.

You'll find it easier to work with a dog that's not brimming with untapped energy. A well-exercised dog makes a better student.

faster than average dogs. On the Mini owner's side is the fact that this breed loves to spend time with its owner and thrives on affection and attention. If you show your Mini love, there's nothing he won't do for you.

KEEP IT POSITIVE

Positive training techniques have become the most acceptable approach to train a dog. Essentially the main principle is that any behavior that results in a reward tends to increase, and any behavior that does not result in reward will decrease. Thus, giving the puppy a tasty treat for a successful behavior makes the puppy want to repeat that behavior. Positive training is a hands-on teaching technique, which means that the trainer has to be ready to reward correct, desirable behavior and also intervene to discourage unwanted behaviors. Whenever a dog does something that is self-rewarding (digging up a flower bed or flinging garbage from the kitchen receptacle, for instance), his fun and tasty discoveries make him "feel good," and he will seek out those thrills again unless deterred by an observant trainer.

CLICK IT GOOD!

A clicker, a positive-training staple to let the dog know a reward is on the way, is used to mark desirable behavior. Essentially, you click to say "good dog" although you don't need an actual clicker, you can just say, "yes" or "good." Most importantly, be consistent in what you choose to do (click or praise) so the signal is clear to the dog.

Timing is everything when it comes to clicking for good behavior. Don't delay too long between the dog's correct behavior and the click, maybe a second or two, and then you should give the reward within five seconds of the click. If you make the dog wait too long, it will take longer for him to learn the behaviors and you'll have to repeat the lesson many more times. A puppy's attention span is minimal, so if you wait too long to give him the treat, his mind will wander, or he will start moving.

Remember that you are only to give the command once. Many new trainers make the mistake of enthusiastically repeating the command. Say "sit" once and mean it. By repeating the command, you're allowing the dog to decide when he wants to execute the behavior. You have to be the one in control, and what you say goes. When teaching come, for example, repeating the word a few times is the worst thing you can do. There may be a moment in life when the dog's obedience to the come command has real consequences. You want the dog to respond immediately without a moment to think about whether he wants to obey yet. To avoid repeating yourself, begin by showing the dog the treat and then give the command/signal in a firm voice. Allow the dog three seconds to respond, and if he does not, simply turn away from the dog, without a word. The dog still knows you have a treat and will likely move his position so he can see you. Show the dog the treat and give the command. If the dog responds (or even partially responds, such as a quick sit or a half sit), click and then give him a treat. Always make sure the dog knows that you are pleased. (Act happy, even if you're not particularly impressed by the dog's performance.) It's hoped that the dog prefers the praise and the treat to being ignored—Minis hate being ignored as much as anyone.

When and where to train are also important considerations. The right place and time can limit the dog's number of mistakes. Working with the dog after a good long walk is better than first thing in the morning when he has a full tank of puppy fuel to burn. Home schooling works better when it's spontaneous and brief. You don't need an extensive lesson plan for your pup. His lessons should be a part of life, so you're best to incorporate them into his everyday life. Practice a sit before you give your puppy his bowl; practice the stay before opening the door to go for a walk; practice the wait/ok before unlatching the door to his crate.

When introducing a new lesson (command), choose a specific time and quiet place, free from distractions. Set aside five minutes to work on a new lesson: this isn't a forty-five-minute period. Brief and positive is the way to go. End the session before the dog gets bored and begins to get fidgety or starts ignoring commands. Once the dog is obeying a new command consistently (say eight out of ten times), then you can introduce some distractions into the environment. If you've been practicing the sit-stay in various rooms of the house, proceed to take the dog in the backyard to practice the behavior. Once the dog performs consistently in a familiar place, somewhere in the house or backyard, then you can try the front yard, sidewalk, or the park. It's critical that your dog obey commands in all environments, but don't rush it.

Did You Know?

Whether you're walking a 100-pound Giant Schnauzer or a 10-pound Miniature puppy, leash training is essential to your own happiness. Walking a dog can be (and should be) a pleasurable experience for dog and owner. Your job is to teach your puppy to walk like a little gentleman or lady on his leash—NOT to yank, pull, and twirl around like a carnival ride. It's no fun getting pulled down the street by an "unbroken" Mini, and it's equally no fun for a dog to be constantly yanked and corrected for misbehaving by his "end-of-your-leash" frustrated owner.

Most Miniature Schnauzers are home-schooled, though they commonly excel in obedience classes since they enjoy the company of other dogs.

NINE LESSONS TO A WELL-BEHAVED MINIATURE SCHNAUZER

Here are the nine basic lessons that you will teach your puppy whether at home or in a puppy class. If you choose to take your Miniature Schnauzer to puppy class, you'll have to practice the lessons at home too. All of these home-schooling lessons add up to a well-behaved dog that will be a pleasure to have around company in your home or out in public. These lessons are also the basis of good manners and all will help your puppy earn the AKC Canine Good Citizen award.

Take it: We begin with the take it command which essentially tells the puppy it's OK to accept a treat or a toy. You practice this by presenting a treat to the puppy, placing it near his nose, and then opening your hand and saying "take it." No puppy ever fails this first lesson, which is why it's a no-fail place to start. You can practice the take it with a toy or a small dumbbell too.

Leave it: This command is the opposite of take it and much harder to teach since it goes against the puppy's will and stomach. Same treat as we used in take it, this time you hold your palm out to the pup, say "leave it." As the puppy attempts to grab it (as he naturally assumes "take" and "leave" are synonyms), you quickly close your hand and repeat "leave it." No puppy likes a lesson that denies him food, but this one necessarily does. To reward the puppy for not grabbing the treat, practice the take it and let him have the treat.

Drop it: The drop it cue is even less popular with dogs than leave it since this lesson denies them something that is already in their mouth. Not likely a treat, but rather an object like half a poinsettia or something they found in the litter box. In order to practice the drop it, you have to start with take it. Have the puppy take a toy from you and then after a few seconds tell him to "drop it." When he releases it, give him a treat and lots of praise. In a real-life situation, when your puppy has something undesirable in his mouth, firmly say "drop it" and then praise him for correctly responding. If the puppy doesn't respond, calmly walk over and remove the object from his mouth as you repeat the drop it command.

Sit: With your Mini on his leash, hold a treat above his head and command "sit" in a strong voice. As the pup looks up toward the treat, he should assume the sit position. Say "good dog" and give him the treat. If the dog doesn't respond the first couple of times, place your hand on his rear quarters and press down gently as you put the treat closer to his nose. He'll get the idea in a couple of licks. Never push hard on the dog's hindquarters.

Come: It's unlikely, but not impossible, that the sit command could save your dog's life, though come very likely can. You can't underestimate the importance of teaching your dog a reliable recall. Begin teach-

Can Your Dog Pass the Canine Good Citizen® Test?

An AMERICAN KENNEL CLUB Program

Once your Miniature Schnauzer is ready for advanced training, you can start training him for the American Kennel Club Canine Good Citizen® Program. This program is for dogs that are trained to behave at home, out in the neighborhood, and in the city. It's easy and fun to do. Once your dog learns basic obedience and good canine manners, a CGC evaluator gives your dog ten basic tests. If he passes, he's awarded a Canine Good Citizen® certificate. Many trainers offer classes, and the test is the "final exam" to graduate. To find an evaluator in your area, go to www.akc.org/events/cgc/cgc_bystate.cfm.

Many therapy dogs and guide dogs are required to pass the Canine Good Citizen® test in order to help as working and service dogs in the community. There are ten specific skills that a dog must master in order to pass the Canine Good Citizen® test:

1. Let a friendly stranger approach and talk to his owner
2. Let a friendly stranger pet him
3. Be comfortable being groomed and examined by a friendly stranger
4. Walk on a leash and show that he is under control and not overly excited
5. Move through a crowd politely and confidently
6. Sit and stay on command
7. Come when called
8. Behave calmly around another dog
9. Not bark at or react to a surprise distraction
10. Show that he can be left with a trusted person away from his owner

In order to help your dog pass the AKC CGC test, first enroll him in basic training classes or a CGC training class. You can find classes and trainers near you by searching the AKC website. When you feel that your Mini is ready to take the test, locate an AKC-approved CGC evaluator to set up a test date, or sign up for a test that is held at a local AKC dog show or training class. For more information about the AKC Canine Good Citizen® Program, visit www.akc.org/events.cgc.

Body Language

ing the come with a tasty treat. Puppies quickly learn to come to their owner for treats or a fun toy, and the come lesson is building on that momentum. Obeying the come command must always yield great things: a treat, a hug, a new squeaky toy. You must never call your dog to you to give him a correction. Place the leash on your Mini so that he knows it's lesson time. Choose a quiet place inside the house to teach this lesson. Begin by kneeling down a few feet from the puppy and say, "Otto, come." When he gets to you, give him a treat and lots of praise. Once he's reliably responding, you can practice without the leash. When you're ready to take the exercise outside (where the blue sky, rustling trees, and all kinds of living things are a distraction), reattach the leash and practice before attempting to do the lesson off-lead.

Stay: Like come, stay can also help you avoid a potential hazard. Telling the puppy to stay at the curb, for example, can keep him from entering a busy road. You can practice the stay with sit, down, or stand, but you can also use it to teach your puppy control. A fine way to practice this basic application is when you open a door. Say "stay" so that the puppy remains standing and doesn't move until you release him with an "OK." The stay command is very helpful when you take your puppy to the groomer or the veterinarian. Start with the puppy on his leash, stand two feet in front of the puppy with a treat in your hand and say "stay." Freeze for a count of five and then step away and say "OK" and give the puppy a treat. Once the puppy is reliably staying for five seconds, you can extend the length of time and the distance from the dog. Puppies destined for the show ring learn the stay command so that they can hold the desired stance (or stacked position). While the puppy is standing and waiting for a treat (as the judge reviews him), he is told to "stay."

Down: Most dogs do not like this exercise, so your job is to make the down the most rewarding of all lessons. Save the puppy's favorite treat for the down exercise. Begin by practicing the sit command, praising the puppy but not giving him a treat for correct responses. With the puppy

Beyond the basic sits and stays, you can teach your Mini fun tricks to entertain your family and friends. This pair is sitting pretty for the camera.

in a sit position, present a treat, keep it a few inches from his nose and then lower it to the floor as you slowly say "dooownnnn." Only when he assumes the correct lying position do you give him the treat and a sedate "good dog." Don't overdo the praise for the down as your excitement will break the mood and the position. If the puppy doesn't respond to the exercise, you can attempt to pull his legs gently forward to lead him to the down position. Never apply pressure on his back or forcibly pull his legs. Since the down is a submissive position for a dog, you can't force it, as that only makes the lesson unpleasant.

Heel: This lesson is called heel because the dog is supposed to walk by your left heel whenever he's walking by your side (with a leash or without a leash). We're not going for that kind of accuracy with a ten-week-old puppy, but the heel lesson is about controlling the puppy and getting him to keep a sensible pace (yours) when he's walking with you.

With the puppy on his leash—and a food reward in your other hand—begin taking a few steps. It's best to be in the house or backyard without too many distractions. Move slowly and talk to your puppy in a calm and encouraging voice. When he's moving at your side, let him sniff and lick the treat so that he will keep pace with you and not race forward. Don't tolerate any jumping up or other antics to get at the food treat. Keep moving and give him your chosen command ("heel," "walk," "let's go" or something else). Don't practice the heel lesson when you're taking the puppy out for a potty visit. You may overload his brain and he'll forget to pee or heel…or both.

Wait: Here's one of your puppy's great manners lessons. The stay lesson is more a "retain your position" command, whereas wait means stop what you're doing until I say "OK." Practice wait as you are placing the puppy's food on the floor or when you are about to place the puppy's lead on his collar. Wait is a great lesson to help keep your puppy's focus on you.

At a Glance ...

Training is not optional, and every owner must commit to the time and effort it requires to teach his Miniature Schnauzer basic commands and manners. The investment of an owner's time will pay off handsomely in a well-behaved companion dog.

Positive-training techniques are the first and only choice of responsible, caring dog owners. Dogs do not respond to punishment or harsh treatment—bet on love and liver to get the job done.

Always begin lessons in a distraction-free location, and keep the lessons short. End on a positive note, with a lesson the puppy aces every time. A puppy's attention span is as reliable as his bladder. Don't overdo schooling and you'll have a more attentive and responsive student.

Create a lesson plan based on the nine exercises described in this chapter, and you're soon to have a smart and reliable Mini in your family.

CHAPTER EIGHT

Feeding the Mini

There are no mysteries to nutrition, it's completely science. Unfortunately there are many mysteries down an aisle of dog food—cans, bags, pouches, logs, and tubes filled with edible dog stuff can be bewildering to the pet owner. Many dog owners think that they can feed their dogs more cost effectively by cooking for dogs and avoiding the pet-food aisle entirely. While it's certainly possible to buy

A Mini fed a properly nutritious diet will be alert and have plenty of energy. If your dog is lethagric or acting off, consider whether you're offering him the best possible diet.

chicken and rice in bulk and save money, the likelihood of providing a balanced diet for your dog is remote. According to the Merck Veterinary Manual website (www.merckvetmanual.com), most homemade diets are too hi-cal and provide too much protein, and the common household sources of meat and carbohydrates (rice, pasta, grains), which are likely of excellent quality, contain too much phosphorus and too little calcium. Calcium deficiency in dogs being fed homemade diets is not uncommon, as are deficiencies in vitamin E, copper, zinc, and potassium.

Balancing the energy in your dog's diet is another factor to consider. We measure energy in calories, which your dog receives from protein, fat, and carbohydrates (not water, vitamins, or minerals). If your Miniature Schnauzer spends most of his day indoors or walking around the backyard, he will require fewer calories than a working dog or a dog that lives in a kennel.

Commercial dog foods generally contain between 8 and 20 percent fat for a puppy food and 5 to 15 percent for adult food. Fat, of course, adds calories to the diet so the food source must be properly balanced with protein so that the dog is receiving the correct amount of amino acids and nitrogen.

WHICH FOOD IS BEST?

When purchasing dog food, begin by reading the label. Manufacturers are required to provide the ingredient list, product analysis, and nutritional adequacy statement. Based on dry weight, the ingredients are listed in

descending order, which means that the "named protein" should be first: a lamb and rice dinner should start with "lamb." While it's comforting to see lamb, chicken, beef, or fish as the first ingredient, there's no way of determining the quality of the protein source from the ingredient list. However, you should avoid the mysterious term "by-products" on the label. If you see the term "meal," it should be as the second ingredient, not the first. *Meal* refers to a form of dehydrated ground protein. Ideally you will see four or five proteins listed before the first fat (usually an oil). In addition to protein sources, you may also see a grain or two, such as barley, rice, or oats, all of which are perfectly healthy for dogs. Some manufacturers separate the grains into categories in order to list them further down the list. If you see rice or corn flour, meal, and gluten, you know the

Guidance from the AAFCO

The Association of American Feed Control Officials (AAFCO) recommends that puppies receive 22 to 25 percent protein, 8 percent fat, plus vitamins and minerals. The requirement for adult dogs is less protein (10 to 14%) and less fat (5%) and the same or higher vitamin amounts. Protein provides the dog with essential amino acids and nitrogen. The AAFCO vitamin and minerals include calcium, phosphorus, iron, and zinc, and vitamins, including A, D, E, niacin, riboflavin, and thiamine. A sufficient amount of fat and carbohydrates is needed in order for the protein to be converted to energy. Carbs are sugars, starches, and dietary fibers. A dog that is not receiving enough protein will lose both body mass and muscle, have a dull coat, and be generally less healthy.

A PIECE OF HISTORY

From 1927 to 1932, the American Kennel Club recognized the Schnauzer as a single breed, including the Standard and the Miniature, which would compete in separate classes. The judge would then select one dog as "Best Schnauzer" and that dog would continue on to the Group competition. In 1933, the two became separate breeds and competed against each other in the Terrier Group. In 1945, the Standard Schnauzer was moved to the Working Group.

Naturally

An advantage of the natural food craze is that we don't see as much "artificial" stuff in our dogs' food. Avoiding artificial colors, flavors, sweeteners, and preservatives is a good thing. If you're not a chemist and don't recognize the words or acronyms, they're likely not good for your dog. Here's a mini-lexicon of unnatural additives: BHT, BHA, ethoxyquin, sodium metabisulphite, menadione, and dimethyl-primidinol sulfate. Avoid vitamin K, which the FDA bans for human use, but certainly vitamin C and vitamin E are OK. Don't be alarmed by the fancy term *tocopherols,* it's only vitamin E.

manufacturer is hoping you're not doing your homework. Grains are not the same as fillers, so corn bran, rice hulls, or soy meal are not desirable.

The guaranteed product analysis states that the product contains at least the legal minimum of crude fat and crude protein and no more than the legal maximum of crude fiber and water. Since canned food is about three-quarters water, the percentages will be lower than dry foods, which typically contain less than 10 percent water.

The nutritional adequacy statement should say that the food is "complete and balanced," indicating that the manufacturer has met the AAFCO feeding trials requirement for nutrients.

A "complete and balanced" diet will make your Miniature Schnauzer glow from the inside out. His coat, eyes, and attitude will glisten with the signs of good health.

TYPES OF FOOD

The pet food market is dominated by dry foods, the first choice of most dog owners. Dry food presents a number of benefits to the dog owner: it is the most cost-efficient, last the longest, does not require refrigeration, and helps to keep teeth and gums healthy. A piece of dog kibble is essentially meat and meat meal, fats, and grains that are fortified with minerals and vitamins, cooked and then extruded.

Your Mini, however, may prefer canned (or wet) food since it is more palatable and usually contains more meat as well as other protein sources (such as wheat and soy), boosting the food's nutritional value. A can of dog food contains cooked meat and meat meal, combined with water, fat, vitamins and minerals. The manufacturing process to produce canned foods makes this type of food the safest to feed your dog. Canned foods are typically more costly than dry foods.

Semi-most or soft-moist foods contain less water than canned food (only about 35 percent) and, like dry food, do not require refrigeration. This type of food contains more sugar and salt than the other types, which are added to preserve the food and prevent the growth of mold and bacteria. Some owners prefer this type of food for picky eaters, despite the higher price and sugar content. Minis like the taste and it gives them good energy.

LIFE-STAGE FORMULAS

Puppy food…adult food…senior food. It doesn't take much research to know that you are best to feed your Mini puppy a food that has the word "puppy" on the label. Since puppies require higher amounts of protein and fats than adult dogs, a puppy food best meets their nutritional requirements. You can switch to an adult dog food when the Mini is a year old, though it's best to confer with your vet and breeder on this. You can keep the Mini on an adult food until he is eight years of age or older. A healthy, active dog can remain on the adult formula until he is ten years

old. You can start offering the senior formula sooner if your dog becomes less active.

DAILY FEEDING TIMES

Dogs embrace the idea of structure, and a puppy's meals are the perfect frame for their day. When you bring your Mini home at eight weeks of age, he will need to eat three meals a day, essentially breakfast, lunch, and dinner. After about a month, you can replace the lunch meal with

Veggies, Too!

Get your puppy used to eating raw fruits and veggies, such as apple slices, snap peas, or blueberries. A little natural peanut butter on a pear slice would be a fun, special treat. Only offer veggies that you would eat raw: chunks of raw pumpkin or potato are not a good idea. Also, be aware that grapes, raisins, avocados, and nuts should be avoided with dogs.

Puppies expect their owners to provide structure in training, recreation, and mealtimes.

a healthy snack and only offer two full meals a day. This is preferred for the life of the dog, though some owners only feed once a day. With small dogs like the Miniature Schnauzer, two meals works better, for good digestion and overall conditioning.

Utilize mealtimes for training too. By providing your puppy with his scheduled breakfast, lunch, and dinner you're reminding him that you are the source of his care and leadership. Dogs equate food with "the good stuff in life," and you provide all that and a bag of baby carrots.

TREATS, SNACKS, AND PEOPLE FOOD

In order to keep your Mini lean, you'll have to keep an eye on how many treats you offer him on a daily basis. While your puppy is becoming an "A" student, he could become as plump as he is smart! Read the label on treats and consider the calories you're offering your Mini every time he sits pretty. Think outside the box (or package) and give your puppy some healthy treats, such as baby carrots, (unbuttered/unsalted) popcorn, or an unsweetened breakfast cereal.

While we're on the topic of human foods that can be harmful to dogs, be aware that you can kill your dog with love, which is spelled "c-h-o-c-o-l-a-t-e." Dogs cannot tolerate chocolate. Avoid all caffeinated and alcoholic items for dogs, including coffee, beer, and soda. Some dog breeders recommend offering your dog herbal (decaffeinated) tea if he has an upset stomach. Remember to hold the milk with that tea, since many dogs are lactose intolerant.

At a Glance ...

Providing your Miniature Schnauzer with a balanced diet can be as easy or difficult as you decide to make it. Whipping up a homemade dinner for your dog will likely not provide the necessary nutrition needed for proper growth and maintenance.

Selecting a high-quality commercial brand of dog food, either dry, wet, or semi-moist, requires reading the label and a little research. Only offer your Miniature Schnauzer a food that meets your criteria—if he likes the food and eats it with gusto, you're a celebrity chef!

Feed your dog at the same times each day. Young puppies do best on three meals a day. Once your Mini is an adolescent, you can skip the midday meal and replace it with a healthy treat.

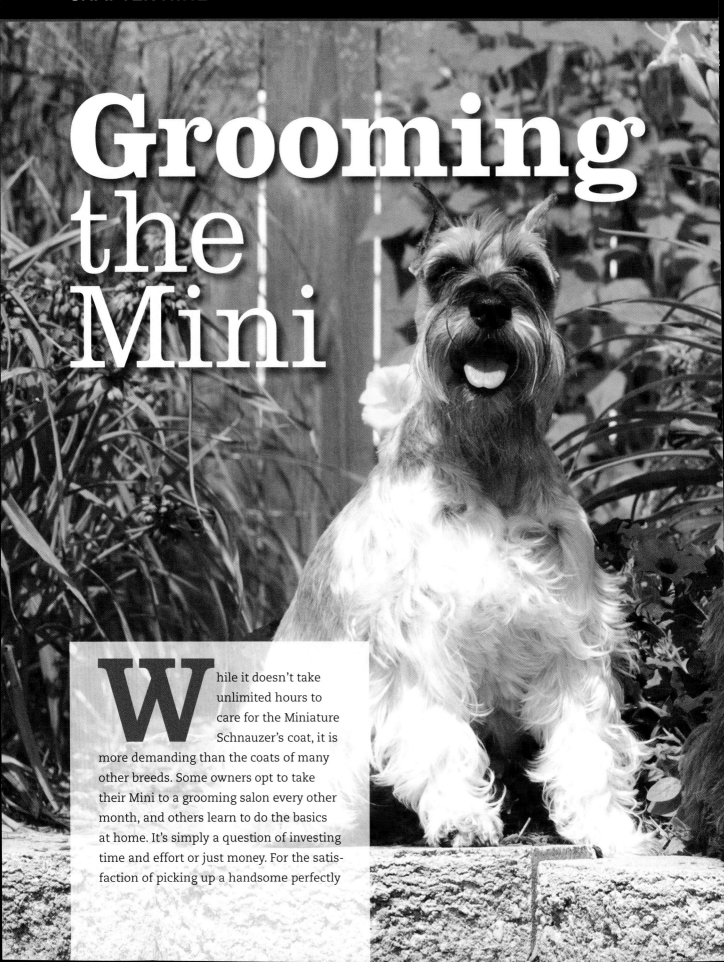

CHAPTER NINE

Grooming the Mini

While it doesn't take unlimited hours to care for the Miniature Schnauzer's coat, it is more demanding than the coats of many other breeds. Some owners opt to take their Mini to a grooming salon every other month, and others learn to do the basics at home. It's simply a question of investing time and effort or just money. For the satisfaction of picking up a handsome perfectly

Make an Appointment

Seek out a professional advice from your breeder or a local grooming shop. Many owners opt to bring their Minis to the grooming salon instead of tackling the process at home. If you're busy and can afford it, then by all means find a reliable salon and enjoy the results of a beautifully maintained Mini. If the grooming salon is in the same neighborhood as your own salon, you can plan both haircuts on the same day!

appointed Mini from the salon, it could be money well spent. For the more industrious and/or thrifty, home grooming is perfectly doable and your Mini will enjoy the time spent with you. Some dogs despise grooming salons, and for their own sake, it's better to keep the grooming tasks at home. It's a personal decision, but what's most important is that you keep your Mini groomed so that his coat doesn't become unruly and tangled.

In addition to the coat, every Miniature Schnauzer will need to have his nails trimmed regularly, his teeth brushed every day or two, and his ears kept clean and free from debris. All of these tasks are easily accomplished by his loving owner and a few supplies from the pet store.

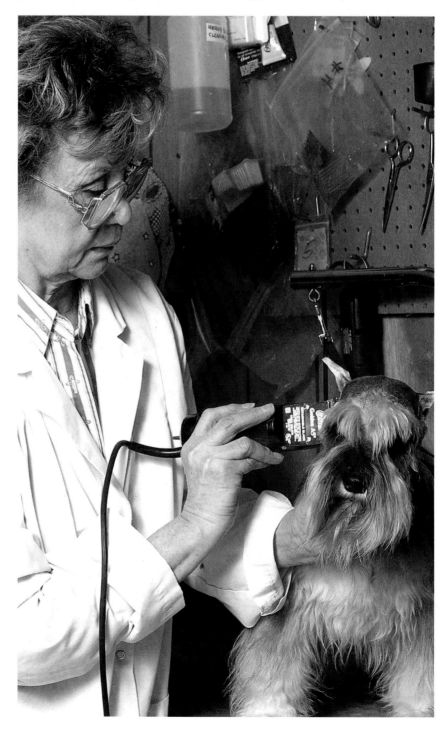

Before picking up a clipper, visit a grooming salon or meet with your breeder to learn how to properly groom your Mini's coat.

TRIMMING THE PET MINI

The coats of pet Minis are maintained by using an electric trimmer, which gives the dog an appropriate silhouette even though the double coat is sacrificed for convenience. Whether maintaining a pet or a show dog, the outline of the dog's coat is the same, and the American Miniature Schnauzer Club offers a diagram on its website to illustrate how each area of the body should be trimmed.

It is possible for a pet owner to learn how to trim his or her Miniature Schnauzer, but it will take time and effort (and a little talent) to master the techniques not to mention train the puppy to stand without fidgeting or fussing. Begin working with your puppy on a grooming table (with an arm and noose). Train him to stand steady, with the noose around his neck. Use treats to encourage him to stand and wait. Brush the puppy coat while he's standing. Teach him to stand on his hind feet confidently, as you hold his front paws. He should be unafraid and comfortable on the table, always trusting you. Practice this every day, extending the length of time with each passing week. It takes nearly an hour for an experienced person to groom an adult Mini's coat, so you're going to have to work diligently on this training.

Give your Mini a bath just prior to clippering. You never want to clip or scissor dirty hair. Select a mild shampoo and use warm water, preferably through a nozzle attachment in your sink or tub. Towel dry the dog's coat, leaving some moisture for the combing. Brush upward as you blow dry on the dog's legs and downward on the chest, beard, and eyebrows. It is more manageable to remove mats from the beard or legs when the coat is still damp. Make sure the coat is dry prior to trimming. A dry shampoo (waterless) is an excellent option if you need to clean just one area of the coat.

Did You Know?

All show Minis are plucked or hand-stripped, which not only maintains the dark tips on the salt and pepper but also preserves the breed's natural hard, wire coat. There is no other way to maintain a show dog's coat than hand-stripping, and the best way to learn the procedure is by working with an experienced Mini handler, breeder, or groomer.

Although a book can never teach you as well as an experienced Mini person, we will outline the basic procedure for trimming a pet Mini. You will need both hands to do this, so if your Mini is still unreliable on the table, you'll need a family member or friend to stand by you and steady your dog (and read the instructions aloud to you).

The thickness and texture of your Miniature Schnauzer's coat will determine which blade you will need to use on the body, usually #10 or #15. Trim with the grain or lay of the hair; by going against the grain, you will get a much closer cut, which may be needed with a dog with a thicker coat. Usually the 7F blade is required for dogs with less coat. Be sure that the blade you select is well oiled before you begin, and keep it oiled so that the clipper doesn't overheat.

Practice the following procedure on your dog without turning the clipper on. This is for you to learn first; once you feel confident, then you can plug it in. With a steady hand, hold the electric clipper with the correct blade against the dog's skin. Slowly and evenly begin moving the clipper with the grain of the hair. To avoid clipper burn and any irritation to the dog's skin, it's advisable to hold the dog's skin taut. Apply a little baby oil to the dog's coat if one area becomes sensitive. Keep the blade flat against the skin, beginning with the base of the skull toward the back of the neck (with the grain toward the tail). You will continue to clipper along the back and down the sides to where the chest drops off. You should stop within an inch or two before the elbows. Trim the sides of the body to this line, leaving a small fringe at the loin.

Correct grooming methods achieve the distinctive Miniature Schnauzer outline. Show dogs are hand-stripped to maintain the desired rough texture of the coat.

Salt and Pepper

The most popular color in the Miniature Schnauzer is the salt and pepper combination, given its unique look by the banded hair. A banded hair is darker on the tip and the root, with the coloration becoming lighter between the tip and the root. As a result of this special hair, a salt and pepper Mini must be plucked in order to keep his coloration. An electric clipper, commonly used on pet Minis, will remove the dark tips and make the dog look solid colored.

Use a slicker brush to keep facial furnishings clean and tangle-free.

Ears: A commercially prepared ear-cleaning solution, applied with a cotton ball, will keep ears fresh smelling and wax-free. This can be done once a week.

Eyes: Wipe out eyes with a moistened cotton ball to remove any debris.

Teeth: A toothpaste and brush made for dogs will help keep your Mini's smile bright and his breath good-smelling. Hard bones and treats also assist to keep the teeth tartar-free.

Nails: Using a guillotine-type nail clipper, keep the Mini's nails short and close to his foot. It's always easier to trim nails after the dog's had a bath.

Coat: Brush the coat daily for a minute or two to keep the furnishings from matting and to minimize shedding.

Now clipper down the side of the rear legs to about three fingers above the hock (ankle). Using your other hand, hold the leg furnishings to avoid accidently clippering them off. With scissors or #40 blade, trim hair between pads but not between toes.

Continue now by trimming the forechest, clippering down to where the forechest drops off and the front leg begins. With your scissors, cut hairs on underarms and trim hair upward at a 45 degree angle from the front pads. The hair on the legs should be as dense as possible, which means less is more. Using a straight scissors, you can trim in a circular fashion to give the legs a "stove pipe" appearance.

Going against the grain of the hair, using the #15 blade, clipper the throat and cheek to the dimple. For the top of the dog's head, you'll want to use the #10 blade, clipping against the grain, creating a diamond shape between the eyes. Don't ever shave the bridge of the dog's nose. The desired Miniature Schnauzer skull is "strong and rectangular," sometimes described as brick-like. Groomers strive for a flatness to the skull and cheeks to achieve the desired length and appearance. When trimming the dog's

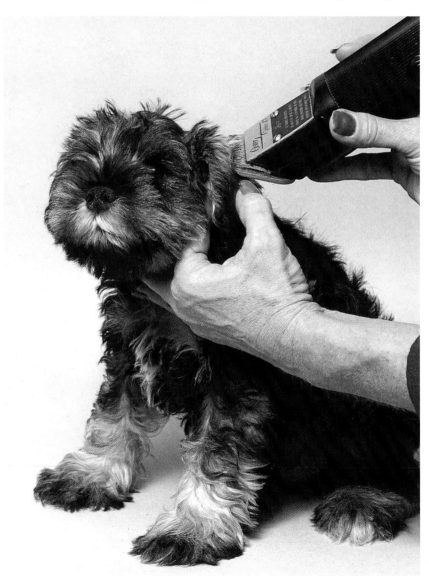

Show pups are only clippered on their ears, face, tummy, and bottom. The coat on the head, neck, and body is handled differently.

face, always be conservative: this beautiful face is unforgiving and you don't want to do anything that will detract from your dog's natural good looks. It's best to consult a professional groomer before trimming the Mini's head.

For the underside of the tail and rear, use the #30 blade and go against the grain. You are not trimming the tail itself, but rather neatening the tail with a scissors to give it a rounded appearance. The tail should not look pointy. Also with the #30, you will trim the dog's belly and underside. Have your Mini stand on his two hind feet while you hold his front feet—a position you should have practiced while his coat was growing weeks ago! Stop trimming at the dog's belly button and avoid the dog's genital region.

To trim the ears, you'll need the #40 blade. For the outside of the ears, go with the grain; for the inside, go against it. You can remove any stray hairs from the ears and ear canal with a tweezers. The inside of the ears is sensitive, so don't overdo it or you'll cause an irritation.

If you're planning to show your dog, ask your breeder to help you find a mentor to assist you in learning the ins and out of hand-stripping and show grooming.

At a Glance ...

Miniature Schnauzers aren't the easiest dogs to groom, especially if you want to keep your Mini looking like a Mini. A good grooming salon might be your chosen path.

∙ ∙

Pet Minis can be groomed with an electric clipper, though this method can alter the color and characteristic rough texture of the coat. Before attempting to clipper your dog yourself, visit a grooming salon and observe a professional groomer. Likewise, you can ask an experienced Mini owner or show handler for assistance. Always clipper on the conservative side: you can always take a little more off.

∙ ∙

Show dogs' coats are maintained by plucking, a grooming method done by hand used to keep the correct crisp quality of the breed's coat. It's best to learn this method from a show groomer before attempting it on your dog.

CHAPTER TEN

Healthy Living

When properly cared for, the Miniature Schnauzer can enjoy a healthy, happy life for up to sixteen years. That's a long commitment for an owner, but one that pays off handsomely with each passing year. Proud dog owners love to boast about how their Minis are fourteen going on fifteen and still acting like a nine year old! With preventive care, a good trusted veterinarian, exercise,

and a balanced diet, your Miniature Schnauzer will be a source of true pride for you and your family.

Starting with a well-bred Miniature Schnauzer, of course, is the most sensible first step. Always put your money on the best horse, or dog, as the case may be. Your next step is to locate a qualified veterinarian in your area. A good vet can help you to become the best possible dog owner you can be. The third step to maintain a healthy, happy dog is for you to work diligently to know your dog. A good dog owner instantly recognizes when his or her dog is feeling off and knows what to look for.

VISIT THE VET

Start looking for your veterinarian as soon as you decide upon a puppy. Hopefully this will give you at least six weeks to conduct a search for a qualified veterinarian. If you live in a heavily populated area, such as a suburb or city, there should be many good options. Rural dog owners may have fewer choices for pet vets within reasonable driving distance. Take the time to visit a few different clinics and talk to the staff and meet the vet. You're looking for a vet who makes you feel confident and at ease, someone whom you feel comfortable talking to and who speaks to you in a knowledgeable but understandable and personable way.

If your breeder has placed dogs in your area before, he or she may have a recommendation. You should also reach out to friends and neighbors who own dogs to find out who they use and whether or not they're happy with the services. Only seek out opinions from people you trust.

As realtors always say, "location, location, location," and finding a vet

CORE Vaccines
Check with your vet, but all puppies should receive vaccines for the following diseases:

CONDITION	TREATMENT	PROGNOSIS	VACCINE NEEDED
ADENOVIRUS-2	No curative therapy for infectious hepatitis; treatment geared toward minimizing neurologic effects, shock, hemorrhage, secondary infections	Highly contagious and can be mild to rapidly fatal	Recommended (immunizes against adenovirus-1, the agent of infectious canine hepatitis)
DISTEMPER	No specific treatment; supportive treatment (IV fluids, antibiotics)	High mortality rates	Highly recommended
PARVOVIRUS-2	No specific treatment; supportive treatment (IV fluids, antibiotics)	Highly contagious to young puppies; high mortality rates	Highly recommended
RABIES	No treatment	Fatal	Required

Select a veterinarian who lives relatively close to your home and who has experience with small dogs like the Miniature Schnauzer. A good vet will guide you toward the best possible preventive health plan for your dog.

A PIECE OF HISTORY

Ch. Dorem Display, bred by Dorothy Williams and owned by Mr. and Mrs. Phil Meldon, is recognized in the Miniature Schnauzer world as the pillar of the modern breed. This remarkable sire did more than make the history books, there's one written about and titled after him: Dan Kiedrowski's 1997 breed book, *The New Miniature Schnauzer: The Breed Since Ch. Dorem Display*. Dorem was the breed's first winner of a Best in Show, an honor he won at the Lackawanna Kennel Club in 1946. He would go on to win four more Bests in Show in his career. Whelped on April 5, 1945, Dorem sired forty-two champions. Although Dorem died over a half century ago, his influence on today's Miniature Schnauzer continues as it is believed that his blood can be found in all Miniature Schnauzer breeding stock around the world.

For the sake of your dog's ongoing health, be proactive and informed. Veterinarians prefer their clients to be knowledgeable and responsible dog owners.

close enough to your home is a huge part of the decision. In case of an emergency, you'll need to get to the vet swiftly. An extra twenty minutes can be a deal breaker when making your final decision. Also be sure that the vet has experience with small dogs, which is common in the suburbs and city but less so in the country.

Miniature Schnauzers are fun, outgoing dogs who should enjoy traveling around with you, so a visit to the vet should be just one more place for him to meet people. Arrange for your puppy's first vet visit within a few days of taking the puppy home.

EXAMS AND VACCINATIONS

Your breeder should have provided his or her puppies with initial vet visits for checkups, booster shots, and wormings. The breeder should provide you with the relevant paperwork to present to your vet so he or she knows how to proceed with vaccinations and parasite prevention. The puppy's first exam should begin with a general exam for the vet to determine the puppy's overall condition, checking his heart, lungs, coat, ears, and mouth to ensure that there aren't any health issues to concern you. Most vets require a stool sample at the first visit so that they can be sure that the puppy is free of internal parasites such as roundworms or hookworms. Because parasites are routinely transferred by the dam to her puppies, breeders have their puppies wormed as a matter of routine.

The vet will also set up a vaccination schedule for the puppy, based on the information you provide. Vaccination schedules vary slightly from place to place, and your vet should be able to advise you about any particular risks dogs face in the area. Veterinarians differ on which vaccines are necessary and the frequency of boosters. The initial vaccination schedule takes up until the pup is sixteen weeks old, after which the dog only needs annual boosters. Your vet will likely send you a reminder notice for boosters and follow-up appointments.

The American Veterinary Medical Association (AVMA) recommends that adult dogs be vaccinated every three years instead of annually, although the rabies vaccination is regulated by state and your vet will know the requirement. The four AVMA core vaccines are canine distemper, canine parvovirus, canine adenovirus (type 2), and rabies, all of which are highly recommended to protect your Miniature Schnauzer

Other Vaccines and Treatment
Depending on where you live and your dog's needs, the following ailments and diseases can be treated through your veterinarian:

CONDITION	TREATMENT	PROGNOSIS	RECOMMENDATION
BORDETELLA (KENNEL COUGH)	Keep warm; humidify room; moderate exercise	Highly contagious; rarely fatal in healthy dogs; easily treated	Optional vaccine; prevalence varies; vaccine may be linked to acute reactions; low efficacy
FLEA AND TICK INFESTATION	Topical and ingestible medications	Highly contagious	Preventive treatment highly recommended
HEARTWORM	Arsenical compound; rest; restricted exercise	Widely occurring infections; preventive programs available regionally; successful treatment after early detection	Preventive treatment highly recommended; treating an infected dog has some risks
INTESTINAL WORMS	Dewormer; home medication regimen	Good with prompt treatment	Preventive treatment highly recommended
LYME DISEASE (BORRELIOSIS)	Antibiotics	Can't completely eliminate the organism, but can be controlled in most cases	Vaccine recommended only for dogs with high risk of exposure to deer ticks
PARAINFLUENZA	Rest; humidify room; moderate exercise	Highly contagious; mild; self-limiting; rarely fatal	Vaccine optional but recommended; doesn't block infection, but lessens clinical signs
PERIODONTITIS	Dental cleaning; extractions; repair	Excellent, but involves anesthesia	Preventive treatment recommended

Know Your Dog

An owner who knows his dog's behavior, personality, and appearance will recognize when something's not quite right. Here's a quick reference list of things to watch for in your Miniature Schnauzer:

SEE THIS	NOT THAT
Moist, black nose	Crusting or dryness
Freedom of movement	Favoring one side over the other, limping, wobbling, or tentative steps
Clean and pink ears	Discharge, waxy buildup, or foul odor
Shiny, resilient coat	Lackluster coat, flea droppings, or actual tiny bugs
Pink gums and white teeth	Bad-smelling breath or sore teeth
Bright, clear eyes	Discharge, gunk, or cloudiness
Eating and drinking normally	Fussiness, excessive thirst, diarrhea, or loose or bloody stool
A discernible waist	Plumpness, roundness
Overall fitness	Weakness or reluctance to exercise

against contagious and potentially lethal diseases. All four of these diseases affect puppies and adult dogs. The rabies immunization is required by law in all fifty states, and documentation of rabies inoculation is required in most municipalities to obtain a local dog license.

AVMA also lists noncore vaccines, including measles, Bordetella bronchiseptica (more commonly called kennel cough), canine parainfluenza virus, canine influenza virus, leptospirosis interrogans, canine coronavirus, and Lyme disease (borreliosis). These are recommended only in particular circumstances where risk is believed to be present.

DENTAL CARE

Although daily tooth brushing is recommended by vets, most owners prefer to brush teeth every other day or twice a week. That may not be ideal, but it's better than monthly or yearly! Tooth brushing promotes good clean teeth and gums of course, but also a strong heart and a longer life. Early loss of teeth and tartar buildup are of great concern to Mini owners. And don't forget, fresh breath! Every time your Mini smiles at you or pants in your face, you'll be glad that you've spent the time to brush his teeth. Infection in your dog's gums can lead to other health

Keep your Miniature Schnauzer smiling. Clean white teeth and fresh breath are the signs of a healthy, well-kept dog.

problems, and plaque and tartar buildup in the mouth can pollute your dog's whole system. Invest in a doggy toothbrush and paste and get your dog in the habit of sitting politely for his special tooth-care time.

In addition to brushing your Mini's teeth, provide him with hard chew toys, such as nylon bones or rawhide, as well as hard biscuits and kibble, all of which serves to clean the teeth.

BUGS AND WORMS

Fleas may be a part of life, and scientists assure us that these pesky parasites have been around since the days of the dinosaurs. Lucky for us, our

Support Canine Health Research

The mission of the American Kennel Club Canine Health Foundation, Inc. (AKC CHF) is to advance the health of all dogs by funding sound scientific research and supporting the dissemination of health information to prevent, treat, and cure canine disease. The foundation makes grants to fund a variety of health efforts:

- Identifying the cause(s) of disease
- Earlier, more accurate diagnosis
- Developing screening tests for breeders
- Accurate, positive prognosis
- Effective, efficient treatment

The AKC CHF also supports educational programs that bring scientists together to discuss their work and develop new collaborations to further advance canine health.

The AKC created the foundation in 1995 to raise funds to support canine health research. Each year, the AKC CHF allocates $1.5 million to new health-research projects.

How You Can Help: If you have an AKC-registered dog, submit his DNA sample (cheek swab or blood sample) to the Canine Health Information Center (CHIC) DNA databank (www.caninehealthinfo.org). Encourage regular health testing by breeders, get involved with your local dog club, and support the efforts to host health-education programs. And, if possible, make a donation.

For information, contact the AKC Canine Health Foundation, P.O. Box 900061, Raleigh, NC 27675-9061 or check out the website at www.akcchf.org.

Give your Miniature Schnauzer plenty of opportunities to stay trim. Exercise is a vital component in every dog's health plan.

modern science provides us with excellent preventive measures to rid our lives of this creepy critters, technology our caveman forebears and the family wolf would have cherished.

If your Miniature Schnauzer is going to spend any time outdoors—and we hope he is—it may not be feasible or possible to protect him from fleas and ticks entirely. If your Mini plays in your backyard daily, it's a good investment to have your lawns treated by a landscaper for fleas and ticks in the spring and fall as necessary.

Ridding your world of fleas is completely doable and requires that you kill the fleas inside the home (and yard) as well as on the dog. Modern technology is a wonderful thing, and the development of insect-growth regulators (IGR) and safe insecticides have effectively eradicated our dogs' flea infestations. The IGR consists of a spray to use around the home (including furniture, rugs, corners and crevices in the floor, etc.) and a liquid to apply on the dog (usually on the dog's coat behind his neck, where he can't reach it) or a pill. Your vet has lots of experience in killing fleas, so discuss the best options with him or her prior to making any investments.

A Visit to the Dentist

When your Mini is six months old, your vet can give him a thorough dental evaluation to assess whether or not all his adult teeth have properly emerged. Puppies lose their deciduous teeth as they grow up, and you may find them in his bed or crate or on the floor. It's no reason for concern, but the doggy tooth fairy retired ages ago!

Second only to fleas are ticks, which carry potential diseases to your dog. The infamous deer tick is the source of the dreaded Lyme disease (borreliosis), which affects humans as well as dogs and is notoriously difficult to diagnose conclusively. Dermacentor ticks spread Rocky Mountain spotted fever and Colorado tick fever, and the brown dog tick causes ehrlichiosis or rickettsiosis.

Internal parasites include a host of nasty nematodes: namely roundworms, tapeworms, hookworms, whipworms and heartworms. Commonly puppies inherit roundworm larvae from their dams, along with their good looks and personality. Worming usually rectifies this infestation, and your vet will confirm that by a stool sample at the first puppy visit. Signs of worms in your Mini include diarrhea, bloody or mucousy stools, weight loss, flaky, dry hair, and general poor condition. If you suspect a worm infestation, bring a stool sample to your vet immediately. Heartworm, on the other hand, is a completely different monster and its presence is determined by a blood test. Monthly preventatives will protect your dog from the onset of this extremely debilitating disease.

A SIMPLE CHOICE

The American Kennel Club recommends that all pet owners who have no intention of participating in conformation dog shows spay or neuter

There's no limit to the Mini's talents, as this budding sand architect proves. Always check the feet and pads after a visit to the beach.

Plan to have your pet Mini spayed or neutered once he or she's fully mature. Discuss the timing of this surgery with your vet.

their Miniature Schnauzers. Veterinary studies indicate that spaying and neutering are the best way to ensure that your dog live a longer, disease-free life. It's very likely that your breeder insists upon spaying and neutering your Miniature Schnauzer and that this stipulation is in the seller's contract. Breeders frown upon owners breeding their Minis for any reason other than to improve the breed. But if you decide that you are interested in breeding your Miniature Schnauzer bitch, discuss this with your breeder. He or she can serve as a great mentor to you and will be happy to make recommendations about getting involved with showing your dog, meeting other breeders and exhibitors, and finding a suitable stud dog for your bitch.

At a Glance ...

The greatest investment you can make in your Miniature Schnauzer is his healthcare. Starting out with a well-bred Mini is the obvious first step, and finding a reliable veterinarian is the second.

. . . .

Your vet will advise you about the necessary vaccinations required and recommended for your Miniature Schnauzer based on your dog's age and the area in which you live.

. . . .

Parasites—internal and external—are a nuisance that dog owners often have to face. Thanks to veterinary science, all of these bugs and worms are easy to prevent and/or eradicate. Let your vet lead the way to a happy pest-free existence for your Mini.

. . . .

Don't hesitate to have your Miniature Schnauzer spayed or neutered: it's the smartest and safest option for the health of your dog and for the good of dogs everywhere.

CHAPTER ELEVEN

Just Do It!

An active Miniature Schnauzer is a healthy and happy Miniature Schnauzer. Whether you've got your sights set on red, white, and blue ribbons, a silver Best in Show trophy, or a champion title, there's a whole world of rewards out there for every dog and owner. Not every owner has a strong competitive spirit or the desire to walk into a show ring, but at the very least, every dog owner should want to

put a leash on his or her dog and walk out the front door! Exercise, fresh
air, and new places and people will keep you and your Mini smiling and
energized. Thanks to the American Kennel Club, there's a whole world of
dog activities for the super smart Miniature Schnauzer and his dedicated
owner to enjoy.

DOG SHOWS

Not a new organization in the dog world by a long shot, the American Kennel Club has been around for well over a century, having been
established in 1884. If you haven't seen signs in your community for a
local AKC dog show, you've probably not been looking for one. Each year
the AKC sponsors about four thousand dog shows—that's an average of
eighty in each state! Not all dog shows, however, are the size of the ones
you see on television on Thanksgiving Day (filmed earlier in the year
in Philadelphia, PA) or the AKC's own annual extravaganza, the AKC/

Eukanuba National Championship Show, which has become the nation's largest with about 4,000 dogs entered each year.

Miniature Schnauzers are natural show dogs because they love being the center of attention. Showing off is one of the Mini's god-given talents. While dog shows are serious competitions in which judges determine which dogs are the best, there is still an obviously degree of showmanship required, from both the dog and the handler.

If you've heard dog shows referred to as conformation shows, this term stems from the idea that the judge is looking at the dogs to determine which one mostly closely conform to his breed's standard. The standard describes the imaginary perfect dog of a specific breed, and the judge is trying to find the one who gets closest to that elusive dog. When Miniature Schnauzers are competing against other Miniature Schnauzers—at the Breed level—the judge's winner is called the Best of Breed. The judge will also select a Best of Opposite Sex, meaning the runner-up of the opposite sex. Since dog shows were originally designed as a forum to determine which dogs are the most fit for breeding, the Best of Opposite Sex award is obviously very important.

After the Minis finish the Breed judging, the Best of Breed goes on to compete in the Group, and the Miniature Schnauzer is a member of the Terrier Group. A different judge is assigned the Group competition, and he or she selects four winners, placed first through fourth.

At an all-breed show, all seven Group winners will then compete, usually under a different judge, for the ultimate award, Best in Show, as well as a Reserve Best in Show.

Junior Showmanship

AMERICAN KENNEL CLUB®

Junior Showmanship classes at dog shows, open to children ages nine to eighteen years old, offer the opportunity for budding fanciers to develop their handling skills and learn about good sportsmanship, dogs, and dog shows. The competitions include handling and performance events, similar to those offered for adults. Judges evaluate the children's handling methods, rather than the animals, although the dogs do need to be registered with the AKC. If your child shows interest in Junior Showmanship, encourage it! Many junior handlers continue in their love of dogs to become professional handlers, veterinarians, breeders, and trainers. Learn more about the Junior Showmanship program at www.akc.org/kids_juniors.

Did You Know?

Earthdog events were sponsored by the American Working Terrier Association in 1971 to encourage the owners of go-to-ground terriers and Dachshunds to hunt with their dogs. A couple of decades later, the American Kennel Club decided to gets its paws dirty and began to sponsor earthdog tests. The first AKC earthdog test took place on October 1 and 2, 1994. The Miniature Schnauzer was not eligible to participate in these activities until 2001 when the breed was added to the list of eligible breeds.

If you're interested in showing your Miniature Schnauzer, visit the AKC website to find local shows in your area. Visit a couple of shows without your dog, and get an idea of how the show procedure works. Introduce yourself to other Mini handlers and watch them groom, practice, and handle their dogs. Once you decide that you're confident enough to enter your dog, you and your dog will have an advantage. Novices frequently don't prepare for the first time in the ring, and their dogs can instantly sense their owners' insecurity and fear. You have to make the dog's first experiences in the ring fun and positive. Remember, you are a winner just for being there! At least, that's what you want your perceptive Mini to believe, and he will!

PERFORMANCE EVENTS

The AKC offers dozens of different performance events for purebred and mixed breed dogs, from obedience and field trials to agility and Rally-O. There's also tracking tests and, for terriers, earthdog tests.

Although obedience trials and tracking have been around the longest, the most popular event is agility trials, which only date back to

1994. In the first two decades of agility trials, they have surpassed obedience trials seven to one!

The allure of agility is that it is as fun to perform as it is to watch: it's essentially a timed obstacle course for dog and handler. Visit a dog show that offers an agility trial so you can witness the excitement. The obstacles vary on every course, but usually include the cat walk, weave poles, collapsible tunnels, jumps through hoops, and the pause table.

Obedience trials, however, are the bread and butter of dog training, the practical extension of obedience lessons and the Canine Good Citizen test. Dog and handler must work closely, using voice commands and hand signals. The exercises in an obedience trial include the long stay, hurdles, long jump, sitting in a group, as well as scent discrimination, the latter points the way to tracking tests. Obedience trials require utter precision and dogs are judged on how perfectly they execute each exercise.

If you're interested in taking a stab at obedience or agility trials, visit the AKC website to locate a training group near your home. Agility training groups will have access to various equipment and the obstacles

The collapsible tunnel is a standard obstacle on an agility course and one of the audience's favorites!

Puppy Sweepstakes Classes

Miniature Schnauzer owners can enter their puppies in puppy and junior sweepstakes classes at the AMSC national specialty. Puppy sweepstake classes are for puppies between six and under twelve months of age, and junior classes are for puppies twelve months and under eighteen months of age. Start your puppy show dogs as early as possible!

needed to get started, and there's no substitute for working with experienced agility handlers to prepare for these fast-paced trials.

Both obedience and agility trials are divided into classes, increasing in difficulty, from Novice to Open to Excellent. Dogs can earn various titles in each class.

Less intense and demanding than obedience and agility trials is AKC Rally-O, a sport that was devised to resemble the rally style of car racing. Happily less precise than obedience trials and super quick like agility, Rally is all about teamwork. This sport sets dogs and handlers

In the Open Class, dogs, working off lead, must retrieve a dumbbell as a part of the required exercises.

The AKC Code of Sportsmanship

- Sportsmen respect the history, traditions, and integrity of the sport of pure-bred dogs.
- Sportsmen commit themselves to values of fair play, honesty, courtesy, and vigorous competition, as well as winning and losing with grace.
- Sportsmen refuse to compromise their commitment and obligation to the sport of purebred dogs by injecting personal advantage or consideration into their decisions or behavior.
- The sportsman judge judges only on the merits of the dogs and considers no other factors.
- The sportsman judge or exhibitor accepts constructive criticism.
- The sportsman exhibitor declines to enter or exhibit under a judge where it might reasonably appear that the judge's placements could be based on something other than the merits of the dogs.
- The sportsman exhibitor refuses to compromise the impartiality of a judge.
- The sportsman respects the American Kennel Club's bylaws, rules, regulations, and policies governing the sport of purebred dogs.
- Sportsmen find that vigorous competition and civility are not inconsistent and are able to appreciate the merit of their competition and the efforts of competitors.
- Sportsmen welcome, encourage, and support newcomers to the sport.
- Sportsmen will deal fairly with all those who trade with them.
- Sportsmen are willing to share honest and open appraisals of both the strengths and weaknesses of their breeding stock.
- Sportsmen spurn any opportunity to take personal advantage of positions offered or bestowed upon them.
- Sportsmen always consider as paramount the welfare of their dogs.
- Sportsmen refuse to embarrass the sport, the American Kennel Club, or themselves while taking part in the sport.

on a course of ten to twenty signs, each of which gives a direction like "Stop and Down," "Slow Forward From Sit," and "Double Left About Turn." Rally is a good stepping stone to agility, and dogs can begin competing at six months of age. Agility trials require the dogs to be one year of age to begin competition.

EARTHDOG TESTS

Digging and chasing vermin is the natural pursuit of most of the breeds in the AKC Terrier Group. Designed for the Terrier Group, these tests cater to dogs that were bred to pursue their quarry underground, in dens or tunnels. In addition to the low-legged terriers, the Dachshunds are also allowed to compete. The purpose of the earthdog test is for the Miniature Schnauzer to display his ability to follow game and work quarry underground. Ideally, the dog shows interest in the quarry (usually a pair of caged rats) by barking, scratching, and digging. Tests are run at various levels of difficulty, and titles such as Junior Earthdog (JE), Senior Earthdog (SE), and Master Earthdog (ME) are awarded to qualifying dogs.

THERAPY WORK

The good nature of the Miniature Schnauzer can be shared with people outside your friends and family by getting involved in therapy work. Registered therapy dogs can visit the residents and patients at nursing homes, hospitals, and senior-care centers. Many Miniature Schnauzer

Tips for Training a Show Dog

- Each time you groom your Mini on his table, make him stand squarely on his four feet.
- Practice the stay while holding his head and tail up when he's on the table.
- Touch your dog's mouth frequently to desensitize him for the teeth exam in the ring.
- Encourage your friends to touch your dog's mouth, feet, and testicles (if he's a male) when he's on the table.
- Once the puppy is walking nicely on a regular lead, introduce the show lead (which is a simple nylon lead with a slip noose for the neck).
- Practice gaiting (walking at an even pace) around the yard with the show lead on.
- Practice stacking your dog—standing straight on all fours—and hold a treat (called bait in the show ring) a few inches from his nose. After he stands for ten seconds, give him a taste of the bait, and then make him wait another ten seconds for a second nibble.

WESTMINSTER KENNEL CLUB

Few would argue that the Terrier Group is one of the most competitive groups at dog shows, but the Miniature Schnauzer's success at the famous Westminster Kennel Club dog show pales in comparison to many other terriers. Only one Mini has won the Group at Westminster: Dorem Display in 1947. Dorem was the first Miniature Schnauzer to win a Best in Show, though not at Westminster in 1947 when he was beaten by the Boxer, Ch. Warlord of Mazelaine, selected by judge David Wagstaff. As of 2012, the Mini has placed in the Westminster Group eight times, which is quite modest compared to sixty-six places for the Terrier king of Westminster, the Wire Fox Terrier. (The Wire Fox ties the Pekingese for most Group placements, which has also placed sixty-six times!) With eight Group placements, however, the Mini has still bested a dozen Terriers at Westminster.

owners believe this to be the most rewarding pursuit for any dog and owner, exceeding even a Best in Show ribbon. Notably many famous Best in Show winners have retired from conformation competition to become goodwill canine ambassadors as registered therapy dogs. A well-socialized and obedience-trained Miniature Schnauzer is an excellent candidate for therapy work.

The best place to start your pursuit of therapy work is to train your dog for the Canine Good Citizen test, which has become the gold standard for most therapy-dog registries. Once your dog becomes registered and starts to make regular visits, he is eligible for the AKC title of Therapy Dog. The AKC Therapy Dog program awards this title to any registered therapy dog that performs a certain number of visits per year. AKC works with over fifty-five organizations that register therapy dogs, including Bright and Beautiful Therapy Dogs, Pet Partners Program (formerly the Delta Society), Therapy Dogs Inc., and Therapy Dogs International. For more information about these organizations and the AKC program, visit www.akc.org/akctherapydog.

At a Glance ...

Get active and involved with your Miniature Schnauzer by investigating the many fun opportunities offered by the American Kennel Club for owners of all dogs.

. . . .

The AKC sponsors thousands of shows and trials around the country each year, on virtually every weekend of the year (and many weekdays).

. . . .

A Miniature Schnauzer who's entered the AKC S.T.A.R. Puppy Program and received his Canine Good Citizen title is ready to try his paw at obedience, rally obedience, and agility trials or even to become a registered therapy dog.

. . . .

Whether you're interested in conformation dog shows, obedience or agility trials, earthdog tests, or therapy work, your Mini is an ideal candidate. Nothing holds a Mini back from accomplishing a task set before him, except, of course, an owner who doesn't embrace adventure. Just do it, and your Mini will too.

Resources

BOOKS

The American Kennel Club's Meet the Breeds: Dog Breeds from A to Z, 4th edition (Irvine, California: I-5 Press, 2014) The ideal puppy buyer's guide, this book has all you need to know about each breed currently recognized by the AKC.

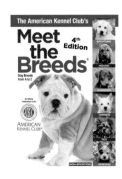

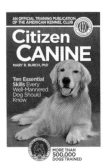

The Complete Dog Book, 20th edition (New York: Ballantine Books, 2006) This official publication of the AKC, first published in 1929, includes the complete histories and breed standards of 153 recognized breeds, as well as information on general care and the dog sport.

The Complete Dog Book for Kids (New York: Howell Book House, 1996) Specifically geared toward young people, this official publication of the AKC presents 149 breeds and varieties, as well as introductory owners' information.

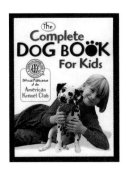

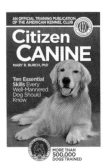

Citizen Canine: Ten Essential Skills Every Well-Mannered Dog Should Know by Mary R. Burch, PhD (Irvine, California: I-5 Press, 2010) This official AKC publication is the definitive guide to the AKC's Canine Good Citizen® Program, recognized as the gold standard of behavior for dogs, with more than half a million dogs trained.

DOGS: The First 125 Years of the American Kennel Club (Irvine, California: I-5 Press, 2009) This official AKC publication presents an authoritative, complete history of the AKC, including detailed information not found in any other volume.

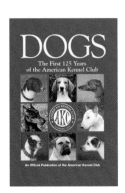

Dog Heroes of September 11th: A Tribute to America's Search and Rescue Dogs, 10th anniversary edition, by Nona Kilgore Bauer (Irvine, California: I-5 Press, 2011) A publication to salute the canines that served in the recovery missions following the September 11th attacks, this book serves as a lasting tribute to these noble American heroes.

The Original Dog Bible: The Definitive Source for All Things Dog, 2nd edition, by Kristin Mehus-Roe (Irvine, California: I-5 Press, 2009) This 831-page magnum opus includes more than 250 breed profiles, hundreds of color photographs, and a wealth of information on every dog topic imaginable—thousands of practical tips on grooming, training, care, and much more.

PERIODICALS

American Kennel Club Gazette

Every month since 1889, serious dog fanciers have looked to the *AKC Gazette* for authoritative advice on training, showing, breeding, and canine health. Each issue includes the breed columns section, written by experts from the respective breed clubs. Only available electronically.

AKC Family Dog

This is a bimonthly magazine for the dog lover whose special dog is "just a pet." Helpful tips, how-tos, and features are written in an entertaining and reader-friendly format. It's a lifestyle magazine for today's busy families who want to enjoy a rewarding, mutually happy relationship with their canine companions.

Dog Fancy

The world's most widely read dog magazine, *Dog Fancy* celebrates dogs and the people who love them. Each monthly issue includes info on cutting-edge medical developments, health and fitness (with a focus on prevention, treatment, and natural therapy), behavior and training, travel and activities, breed profiles and dog news, issues and trends for dog owners. The magazine informs, inspires, and entertains while promoting responsible dog ownership. Throughout its more than forty-year history, *Dog Fancy* has garnered numerous honors, including being named the Best All-Breed Magazine by the Dog Writers Association of America.

Dogs in Review

For more than fifteen years, *Dogs in Review* has showcased the finest dogs in the United States and from around the world. The emphasis has always been on strong content, with input from distinguished breeders, judges, and handlers worldwide. This global perspective distinguishes this monthly publication from its competitors—no other North American dog-show magazine gathers together so many international experts to enlighten and entertain its readership.

Dog World

Dog World is an annual lifestyle magazine published by the editors of *Dog Fancy* that covers all aspects of the dog world: culture, art, history, travel, sports, and science. It also profiles breeds to help prospective owners choose the best dogs for their future needs, such as a potential show champion, super service dog, great pet, or competitive star.

Natural Dog

Natural Dog is the magazine dedicated to giving a dog a natural lifestyle. From nutritional choices to grooming to dog-supply options, this publication helps readers make the transition from traditional to natural methods. The magazine also explores the array of complementary treatments available for today's dogs: acupuncture, massage, homeopathy, aromatherapy, and much more.

Natural Dog appears as an annual publication and also as the flip side of *Dog Fancy* magazine four times a year (in February, May, August, and November).

Puppies USA

Also from the editors of *Dog Fancy,* this annual magazine offers essential information for all new puppy owners. *Puppies USA* is lively and informative, including advice on general care, nutrition, grooming, and training techniques for all puppies, whether purebred or mixed breed, adopted, rescued, or purchased. In addition, it offers family fun through quizzes, contests, and much more. An extensive breeder directory is included.

WEBSITES

www.akc.org

The American Kennel Club (AKC) website is an excellent starting point for researching dog breeds and learning about puppy care. The site lists hundreds of breeders, along with basic information about breed selection and basic care. The site also has links to the national breed club of every AKC-recognized breed; breed-club sites offer plenty of detailed breed information, as well as lists of member breeders. In addition, you can find the AKC National Breed Club Rescue List at www.akc.org/breeds/rescue.cfm. If looking for purebred puppies, go to www.puppybuyerinfo.com for AKC classifieds and parent-club referrals.

www.dogchannel.com

Powered by *Dog Fancy*, Dog Channel is "the website for dog lovers," where hundreds of thousands of visitors each month find extensive information on breeds, training, health and nutrition, puppies, care, activities, and more. Interactive features include forums, Dog College, games, and Club Dog, a free club where dog lovers can create blogs for their pets and earn points to buy products. Dog Channel is the one-stop site for all things dog.

www.meetthebreeds.com

The official website of the AKC Meet the Breeds® event, hosted by the American Kennel Club in the Jacob Javits Center in New York City in the fall. The first Meet the Breeds event took place in 2009. The website includes information on every recognized breed of dog and cat, alphabetically listed, as well as the breeders, demonstration facilitators, sponsors, and vendors participating in the annual event.

AKC AFFILIATES

The **AKC Museum of the Dog**, established in 1981, is located in St. Louis, Missouri, and houses the world's finest collection of art devoted to the dog. Visit www. museumofthedog.org.

The **AKC Humane Fund** promotes the joy and value of responsible and productive pet ownership through education, outreach, and grant-making. Monies raised may fund grants to organizations that teach responsible pet ownership; provide for the health and well-being of all dogs; and preserve and celebrate the human-animal bond and the evolutionary relationship between dogs and humankind. Go to www.akchumanefund.org.

The **American Kennel Club Companion Animal Recovery (CAR) Corporation** is dedicated to reuniting lost microchipped and tattooed pets with their owners. AKC CAR maintains a permanent-identification database and provides lifetime recovery services 24 hours a day, 365 days a year, for all animal species. Millions of pets are enrolled in the program, which was established in 1995. Visit www.akccar.org.

The **American Kennel Club Canine Health Foundation (AKC CHF), Inc.** is the largest foundation in the world to fund canine-only health studies for purebred and mixed-breed dogs. More than $22 million has been allocated in research funds to more than 500 health studies conducted to help dogs live longer, healthier lives. Go to www.akcchf.org.

AKC PROGRAMS

The **Canine Good Citizen Program (CGC)** was established in 1989 and is designed to recognize dogs that have good manners at home and in the community. This rapidly growing, nationally recognized program stresses responsible dog ownership for owners and basic training and good manners for dogs. All dogs that pass the ten-step Canine Good Citizen test receive a certificate from the American Kennel Club. Go to www. akc.org/events/cgc.

The **AKC S.T.A.R. Puppy Program** is designed to get dog owners and their puppies off to a good start and is aimed at loving dog owners who have taken the time to attend basic obedience classes with their puppies. After completing a six-week training course, the puppy must pass the AKC S.T.A.R. Puppy test, which evaluates Socialization, Training, Activity, and Responsibility. Go to www.akc.org/starpuppy.

The **AKC Therapy Dog** program recognizes all American Kennel Club dogs and their owners who have given their time and helped people by volunteering as a therapy dog-and-owner team. The AKC Therapy Dog program is an official American Kennel Club title awarded to dogs that have worked to improve the lives of the people they have visited. The AKC Therapy Dog title (AKC ThD) can be earned by dogs that have been certified by recognized therapy dog organizations. For more information, visit www. akc.org/akctherapydog.

Index

AMERICAN KENNEL CLUB®

Advocating for the purebred dog as a family companion, advancing canine health and well-being, working to protect the rights of all dog owners and promoting responsible dog ownership, the **American Kennel Club:**

Sponsors more than **22,000 sanctioned events** annually including conformation, agility, obedience, rally, tracking, lure coursing, earthdog, herding, field trial, hunt test, and coonhound events

Features a **10-step Canine Good Citizen® program** that rewards dogs who have good manners at home and in the community

Has reunited more than **400,000** lost pets with their owners through the AKC Companion Animal Recovery - visit **www.akccar.org**

Created and supports the AKC Canine Health Foundation, which funds research projects using the more than **$22 million** the AKC has donated since 1995 - visit **www.akcchf.org**

Joins **animal lovers** through education, outreach and grant-making via the AKC Humane Fund - visit **www.akchumanefund.org**

We're more than champion dogs. We're the dog's champion.

www.akc.org